FOLLOWING IN T
OF
KING
ARTHUR

FOLLOWING IN THE FOOTSTEPS
OF
KING
ARTHUR

ANDREW BEATTIE

PEN & SWORD
HISTORY

AN IMPRINT OF PEN & SWORD BOOKS LTD.
YORKSHIRE - PHILADELPHIA

First published in Great Britain in 2020 by
Pen and Sword History
An imprint of
Pen & Sword Books Ltd
Yorkshire - Philadelphia

ISBN 978 1 52672 781 7

Typeset in Ehrhardt MT Std 11.5/14 by
Aura Technology and Software Services, India.

Printed and bound by CPI Group (UK) Ltd, Croydon CR0 4YY

Pen & Sword Books Ltd incorporates the Imprints of Pen & Sword Books
Archaeology, Atlas, Aviation, Battleground, Discovery, Family History, History,
Maritime, Military, Naval, Politics, Railways, Select, Transport, True Crime,
Fiction, Frontline Books, Leo Cooper, Praetorian Press, Seaforth Publishing,
Wharncliffe and White Owl.

For a complete list of Pen & Sword titles please contact

PEN & SWORD BOOKS LIMITED
47 Church Street, Barnsley, South Yorkshire, S70 2AS, England
E-mail: enquiries@pen-and-sword.co.uk
Website: www.pen-and-sword.co.uk

or

PEN AND SWORD BOOKS
1950 Lawrence Rd, Havertown, PA 19083, USA
E-mail: Uspen-and-sword@casematepublishers.com
Website: www.penandswordbooks.com

Contents

Part One

KING ARTHUR: THE LEGEND

King Arthur is the most celebrated of British literary heroes. For over a thousand years he has been immortalised in poetry, prose and art, while more recently his legend has caught the attention of filmmakers and the developers of computer games. Until 2012 there was a children's theme park named after him in Lancashire (which now lies spookily abandoned, awaiting the decision of planners as to what happens to it next). Alongside a tiny coterie of other historical figures – Henry VIII, William the Conqueror, Queen Victoria and Winston Churchill among them – he is one of the larger-than-life personalities from the past who collectively have helped forge Britain's national identity. In fact so deep into the national psyche has Arthur penetrated that the name 'Camelot' serves as the trademark of the UK's National Lottery, who have named the ball-churning machines that select the lottery's winning numbers after Arthur, Guinevere, Galahad, Lancelot and Merlin. More than any other historical figure, Arthur has long reflected how we think about the past, particularly the deep past – and his story has been refashioned, reinvented and retold by virtually every generation. Those who currently claim to be guardians of his 'eternal spirit' are the mystical, Celtic-inspired 'new age' fringes of modern culture that have arisen as a folksy response to the materialism of the present day. The spiritual home of these groups is Glastonbury in Somerset – and it is no coincidence that King Arthur features large in that town's mythology. Yet King Arthur's story is actually everywhere; it is something that everyone 'gets'. Nowhere is this more clearly evinced than in the British children's film *The Kid Who Would Be King*, released in February 2019. The words 'sword' and 'stone' appear nowhere in the title – but the point is that they don't have to; the film's Arthurian theme (here given a contemporary makeover, with bullying at school spicing up the more familiar medieval memes of swords and sorceresses) is instantly recognisable to all. The reason for this is clear. The legend of King Arthur and his knights is integral to what is sometimes called the 'Matter of Britain' – the fundamental building blocks of nationhood that provide the people of Britain with a shared, collective sense of heritage and identity.

For these reasons the bare facts as to who Arthur was – or might have been – are known to virtually everyone; he was the legendary warrior of the early Dark Ages who led the defence of Celtic Britain against the hordes of Saxon invaders in the decades that followed the end of Roman rule. King Arthur gained his legitimacy by drawing a sword from a stone, was invested with magical powers by a wizard named Merlin who was his tutor and guide, and was given a mystical sword named Excalibur by a lady who rose ethereally from the glassy surface of a lake. But what more do we know? Did a warrior-king called Arthur ever actually exist? Or is he an amalgam of several Celtic leaders whose deeds have been blurred into a single figure of legend? Or, is he someone else entirely, a genuine figure of folklore whose exploits were embellished by each generation of bards and wandering storytellers in the early Middle Ages? And how – and, most pertinently to this book, in which locations – does his spirit and legend live on, to be celebrated and revered in a Britain that seems, in troubled times, to be increasingly taking refuge in what are known affectionately as 'the olden days'?

Dark Age Britain: The Historical Background to King Arthur

If a historical figure named Arthur ever lived – and it's unlikely that he did – his exploits would date to the years either side of AD 500, or possibly a little later. This was an era when the institutions of Roman Britain were in full retreat in the face of wholesale Saxon incursions. The precise dates of the Roman abandonment of Britain fall between AD 402 – when archaeological records indicate that the bulk importation of new coinage ceased – and 408, when heavy Saxon attacks on Britain were not repulsed, as by then large numbers of Roman soldiers had been moved to Spain to counter insurgencies there. In the following year a rebellion broke out against the Roman occupiers who remained in Britain. Thereafter power was seized by local potentates, who were drawn variously from landowning and military classes, either Roman or Celtic or, gradually, Saxon. Some scholars are of the opinion that when the Romans left, the social and economic order collapsed; others point out that something resembling Roman (or Romano-British) rule continued in Britain well into the fifth century. The problem is that recorded history effectively stopped in 409; only fragments of text from one or two writers have survived for the two centuries from AD 400 to 600. Archaeological remains are few and far between, and interpreting them has been fraught with controversy. No wonder something monumental has been sucked into the resulting historical vacuum – and that something monumental is the legend of King Arthur and the stories associated with him and his faithful knights. So Arthur is a heroic figure about whom factually we know nothing, and who emerged during an obscure era of history about which we know very little. And this is why he has proved to be such a gift to writers; they can make of him what they will, whether they are a wandering seventh-century bard or a computer games designer from the first quarter of the twenty-first century.

The peoples who moved into Britain during the decades following the departure of the Romans came from modern-day Holland, northern Germany and Jutland (peninsular Denmark). None of these areas had ever come under the yoke of the Romans. But tribes from these areas had been raiding and pillaging the east coast of England since the late third century, so their arrival on the scene in large numbers when the Romans pulled their troops out cannot have been wholly unexpected. One tribe, the Angles, actually gave their name to England; they hailed from the southern part of Jutland (now the German province of Schleswig-Holstein), where to this day an area northeast of the Baltic port town of Schleswig is known as Angeln. But within half a century of the Romans' departure – by, say, the 450s – the tribespeople who crossed the North Sea and pitched up on the beaches of Kent and East Anglia were viewing this new land as a place to live rather than plunder. Britain was sparsely settled and the newcomers found the land could be productively farmed – while the divisions and confusion caused by the withdrawal of the Romans meant that organised resistance was slim. One of the tribes who crossed the North Sea was led by two Saxon brothers, named Hengist and Horsa, whom the Venerable Bede, in his *Ecclesiastical History of England*, tells landed on the shores of Kent in around AD 450 and founded their own kingdom there.

The Venerable
Bede, as depicted
in the Nuremberg
Chronicle of 1493.
(*Source, Wikimedia
Commons*)

Bede died in 735, and so was writing his account of the Saxon settlement of Britain some 300 years after the events he described took place. However, a chronicler named Gildas offers a narrative account of the Saxon incursions that is near-contemporary. It is unclear who Gildas was and where he lived, though according to a chronicle compiled on the Hebridean island of Iona he died in around the year 570. His work *De Excidio Britanniae* (*The Ruin of Britain*) is a 22,000-word commentary on contemporary and recent events in Britain. Gildas's text is more of a sermon, delivered to the people of what he saw to be a Godless Britain, rather than an accurate chronology of events – so his work must be treated with caution. Nonetheless he provides us with some interesting fragments of narrative. For example, Gildas indicates that some groups of Saxons were invited into the country by a 'proud tyrant' (scholars assume this to be the legendary warrior-leader Vortigern) to defend the vulnerable east coast of England against raiders from further afield – but that these Germanic settlers rebelled and attacked their British hosts in the second half of the fifth century. His narrative goes on to describe how many years of inconclusive warfare ensued, culminating in a major British victory against the Saxons in around AD 500 at an unidentified place named Mons Badonicus or Mount Badon (though this did not bring the wars to an end). Yet these events are disputed by many historians, who point out that the archaeological evidence for a time of warfare in the late fifth century (mass graves and male bodies with multiple battle wounds, for instance) is just not there. Instead, these historians maintain that there was no conflict between the Saxons and the Celtic Britons at this time; the Germanic incursions of the fifth century were largely peaceful, and the new settlers intermingled with their hosts, who were of a mindset that was not the nationalist outlook we recognise today but more localised and parochial – and one that would welcome communities being enriched by new blood from outside.

By the early sixth century – the supposed time of Arthur – the Germanic incursions were at their height. Soon all of eastern, south-eastern and central England was ruled by Germanic tribes, who came to be known collectively as the Anglo-Saxons. Gradually these tribes formed themselves into political entities; kingdoms, ruled by warrior kings. This is now the era when everyone agrees that battles erupted, as the leaders of these new kingdoms pushed further into northern and western Britain. One major victory came in 577 at Dyrham in Gloucestershire, which brought the cities of Bath and Gloucester into the Anglo-Saxon fold. But as this violence was unleashed it was joined by a new force, ostensibly preaching peace. Twenty years after the battle at Dyrham, Pope Gregory the Great sent a Roman monk named Augustine to Britain to Christianise the new Anglo-Saxon kingdoms. Augustine came first to Kent, where he converted King Aethelbert and founded a monastery at Canterbury. From there Christianity spread across the new English kingdoms, following the Anglo-Saxons as they expanded their territory. By this time Ireland had already been converted by St Patrick, and missionaries had spread from there into Wales and Cornwall. But not everyone had converted, and at the time of Arthur the British Isles were in a strange limbo with regards to Christianity. This allowed medieval writers to assume that King Arthur was a Christian convert, and so an appropriate hero for their resolutely pious era – but it has also meant that in modern times Arthur has been claimed as a pagan hero, whose followers celebrate him at 'new age' temples such as Stonehenge and ancient healing springs such as those in Glastonbury.

The Origins of the King Arthur Legend (AD 500-800)

By the time of St Augustine, the Celtic Britons had retreated into the extremities of the island of Britain; to Wales and to what is now southwest and northern England. It is these defiant strongholds of the Celts that nurtured the stories of King Arthur. But while the new settlers from across the North Sea recorded their triumphs, the Britons were disinclined to write about their defeats, and in any case had little tradition of written history. Instead, much of the historical tradition of the early Britons was an oral one, and only a tiny part of this was ever committed to writing. In addition, the distinction as we would understand it today between history and literature, between the art of the poet and the scholarship of the historian, was not properly apparent until the twelfth century. Many works that appear to be historical actually incorporate a fair amount of literary and dramatic licence, while many dramatic poems are in fact works that tell of genuine historical events. This has led to the enigma that is Arthur; if he is mentioned in a text, is he a real person or a figment of the author's imagination or a popular figure of folklore? Understanding this tension is vital for anyone who really wants to know how this towering figure in Britain's literary heritage actually came to be.

The earliest surviving manuscript that mentions a Celtic warrior-leader named Arthur is thought to be one that dates from AD 704 and is now kept in the Stadtbibliothek in the city of Schaffhausen in northern Switzerland. The manuscript in question is a life of the Irish saint, Columba. It was written by Adomnán, one of the monks of the monastery that Columba founded on Iona. Soon after its composition this manuscript was brought to continental Europe by another Ioanan monk, named Dorbbene, who came to spread the Christian message among the heathen people who lived around what is now Lake Zurich, which lies just a short distance south of Schaffhausen. In the manuscript we are told that Arthur (named Artúr here) is a famed warrior, the son of the powerful Aedán mac Gabráin, the ruler of Dalriada, an ancient kingdom that grew from its original territory in the north of Ireland to encompass many parts of southwestern Scotland. But Adomnán tells us little about Arthur, beyond the circumstance of his death, which came during a battle with an obscure tribe, the Miathi, a southern Pictish people whose name survives in various place-names around Stirling. This early reference is interesting as it confirms Arthur as a Celtic warrior, but strikingly places him in Scotland rather than south-western England, the principal home of most Arthurian legends – which means that this Arthur might actually have nothing to do with the Arthur that subsequently passed into legend.

This more familiar Arthur – the Celtic hero who hailed from Wales or Cornwall – first emerges in the very early medieval period in various written versions of stories originally told by travelling bards in the great royal courts of Wales and northern England. In these texts Arthur appears as a peerless warrior who was the protector of the Britons against human and supernatural threats; he fights everything from the Saxons to giant cat-monsters and divine boars, which he battles alongside dragons, giants, and witches. (This miasma, where humans make their home in a realm that is part real, part magic, is remarkably similar to that of many modern fantasy novels and games, where princes and kings and castles coexist with other-worldly creatures such as giants and dragons.) In Welsh versions of these tales Arthur has a close connection with the mythical Welsh Otherworld, the realm of deities and the dead that went by the name of *Annwn*, where Arthur launched assaults on fortresses in search of treasure but also sought out a bride for himself. Among these early texts is *Y Gododdin* (*The Gododdin*), attributed to the poet Aneirin, whose origins lie in one of the kingdoms of Yr Hed Ogledd, the name by which northern England and the Scottish Lowlands were known in the Dark Ages, and whose authorship of the poems has been dated to between AD 540 and 640. His poems are preserved in *The Book of Aneirin*, compiled in 1265 – some 700 years after his death – and kept in the Cardiff Central Library. In one stanza Aneirin praises the bravery of a warrior who slew 300 enemies at Catterick in Yorkshire, when armies of a British people known as the Gododdin fought against the Angles during the late sixth century. This particular warrior, we are told, 'glutted black ravens on the rampart of the stronghold, even though he was no Arthur' – that is, his feats cannot compare to those of Arthur. Is this the King Arthur who hailed from Wales or the West Country? Or is it another reference to the 'Scottish' Arthur, Artúr of Dalriada, who appears in the manuscript kept in Schaffhausen? Or is the line in question a later interpolation, added after the historian Geoffrey of Monmouth had done so much to popularise the life and legend of King Arthur in the early twelfth century? If – and it's a big 'if' – Aneirin did really write these lines in the late sixth century, then they are the earliest reference to Arthur that we know of, composed some time before the manuscript now in Schaffhausen.

But Aneirin has a 'competitor' in terms of the earliest-to-mention-King-Arthur stakes. This is his contemporary Taliesin, a shadowy, near-mythical figure who, according to tradition, served for a time as the court poet to the King of Powys. In *Kadeir Teyrnon* (*The Chair of the Prince*) Taliesin makes a reference to 'Arthur the Blessed', while Arthur's expedition to the Underworld is recounted in another poem, *Preiddeu Annwn* (*The Spoils of Annwn*), where Taliesin describes how he accompanied Arthur on an expedition whose goal was to seize the magic cauldron known as the Head of Annwfn. Arthur's valour is also celebrated in *Marwnat vthyr pen* (*The Elegy of Uther Pen*[dragon]), which names Uther Pendragon as Arthur's father. Again, though, the earliest surviving edition of *The Book of Taliesin* dates from the late Middle Ages (and is preserved in the National Library of Wales in Aberystwyth), so the authenticity of these poems as precursors to Geoffrey of Monmouth's work is far from certain.

Arthur is also mentioned numerous times in the Welsh Triads, a collection of short summaries of Welsh tradition and legend which seem to have been written as aides-memoires – reminders of linked stories to prompt bards as they prepared to recite their next tale. The later manuscripts of the Triads are partly derivative of Geoffrey of Monmouth, but the earliest ones show no such influence and are usually assumed to refer to pre-existing Welsh traditions. In these tales, Arthur had become the overlord of Wales, Cornwall and the North of Britain, and his court (specifically described as being in Cornwall) is described as a meeting point of heroes – an early incarnation of Camelot, perhaps. A number of other Arthurian figures also appear in these stories, including Tristan and Iseult (or Isolde) and Merlin, who (along with Taliesin) is a bard in King Arthur's court, though he is not yet recognisable as the wonder-working prophet later presented by Geoffrey of Monmouth.

Arthur in the Literature of the Early Middle Ages (800–1130)

The most important early medieval text that mentions King Arthur is the *Historia Brittonum* (*The History of the Britons*), a purported history of the indigenous people of Britain whose authorship has been traditionally ascribed to Nennius, a monk from Abergele in North Wales who was active in the years around 820. However, both the dating and authorship of *Historia Brittonum* remain subjects of considerable debate. The work is a synthesis of myth and history (though the chronology is often inaccurate), and begins by tracing the origins of the Britons back to a host of historical, mythical and Biblical figures, including Noah's son Japheth, before recounting the fate of the Britons under the Romans and Saxons. The latter are condemned as 'wolves in word and deeds' – but the writer of the *Historia* describes with relish how the Saxons meet their match in the shape of a valiant and ever-victorious warrior named Arthur, who engages with them in twelve battles, though none are assigned actual dates. 'At that time,' the *Historia* maintains,

> the Saxons grew strong by virtue of their large number, and increased in power in Britain ... Arthur along with the kings of Britain fought against them in those days ... His first battle was at the mouth of the river which is called Glein. His second, third, fourth, and fifth battles were above another river which is called Dubglas and is in the region of Linnuis. The sixth battle was above the river which is called Bassas. The seventh battle was in the forest of Celidon, that is Cat Coit Celidon. The eighth battle was at the fortress of Guinnion, in which Arthur carried the image of holy Mary ever Virgin on his shoulders; and the pagans were put to flight on that day. And through the power of our Lord Jesus Christ and through the power of the blessed Virgin Mary his mother, there was great slaughter among them. The ninth battle was waged in the City of the Legion. The tenth battle was waged on the banks of a river which is called Tribruit. The eleventh battle was fought on the mountain which is called Agnet. The twelfth battle was on Mount Badon in which there fell in one day 960 men from one charge by Arthur; and no one struck them down except Arthur himself, and in all the wars he emerged as victor.

Most of these battle sites cannot be identified, though it is thought that the Battle of Badon is one of the battles that might actually have taken place; when and where it was fought, however, is a matter of conjecture. Some of these battles appear in other Welsh sources, though not all are connected explicitly with Arthur, and it has been suggested by some scholars that the author of the *Historia* took this list of battles from a now-lost poem written in Old Welsh which listed Arthur's twelve great victories. This is based on the fact that some of the names appear to rhyme – and that twelve was also a number that in the Middle Ages was invested with mystical properties. Did the writer of the *Historia* 'borrow' battles from the works of other writers to provide a historical context for his central heroic figure? Or has he simply just made them up? Either way it would appear that the *Historia* forms something of a 'bridge' between the mythical Arthur of the Dark Ages and the more historically resonant figure that emerged during the early Middle Ages, though throughout the *Historia* he is described as a *dux bellorum* ('military leader') rather than a king.

Another very early medieval text that attempts to provide a historical chronology of Arthur's life is the *Annales Cambriae* (*The Annals of Wales*). This is the name given to a series of chronicles compiled from diverse sources at St David's in the extreme southwest of Wales. The oldest version of these texts is a twelfth-century copy of what is presumed to be an original that dates to around the middle of the tenth century; it has been suggested that the *Historia Brittonum* was used as a source in its compilation. The chronology presented in the *Annales* is difficult to interpret, but there is a measure of agreement among scholars that year one represents AD 445, so dating Arthur's victory at Badon to AD 516; using this chronology, the fall of both Arthur and his arch-enemy Mordred at the Battle of Camlann can be dated to AD 537, some twenty-one years later. The texts also feature a prophet named Merlin, or more specifically Myrddin Wyllt (Myrddin the Wild), who goes mad and flees into the forest following the Battle of Arfderydd in AD 573. This character was the prototype for Geoffrey of Monmouth's Merlin (who is the basis of the character that everyone knows today), though in the *Annales*, he lives some decades after Arthur and their stories are not connected.

Roughly contemporaneous with the *Annales*, and also originating in South Wales, is a poem entitled *Pa gur yv y porthaur?* (*What man is the gatekeeper?*), found in the so-called Black Book of Carmarthen, a collection of poems written in Welsh from the sixth century onwards and compiled at a priory near Carmarthen in around 1250. This particular poem has been dated to around 1100, but could be considerably older. It takes the form of a dialogue between Arthur and Glewlwyd, the gatekeeper of a fortress he wishes to enter, in which the gatekeeper demands 'What [company] goes with thee?' and Arthur replies, 'The best men in the world.' However, the gatekeeper is suspicious of Arthur. 'Into my house you shall not come, unless you reveal them,' he commands.

So Arthur names his companions as Cei (Kay) and Bedwyr (Bedivere), among others; these are some of the earliest known appearances of these knights in Arthurian literature.

In the centuries that followed the composition of these early medieval texts, King Arthur appeared in the *vitae* ('Lives') that were written of various post-Roman saints. These include the *Life of Saint Gildas*, a biography written around 1100 of the chronicler-saint whose work *De Excidio Britanniae* has already been discussed. The author of the *Life* was a Welsh cleric, Caradoc of Llancarfan. He presents Arthur as the king of the whole of Britain, and narrates how he kills Gildas's brother Huail, as revenge for Huail launching several raids on Arthur's kingdom from what is now Scotland. 'In the hostile pursuit and in a council of war in the Isle of Man [Arthur] killed the young pillager,' Caradoc writes. 'After that slaying the victorious Arthur returned, rejoicing greatly that he had overcome his greatest enemy.' This text also includes an account of Arthur rescuing his wife Guinevere from Glastonbury, where Gildas served in the abbey. A different Arthur is presented in the *Life of Saint Cadoc*, written around 1075

William of Malmesbury, the English historian who believed in the veracity of a historical King Arthur. This window was installed in Malmesbury Abbey in 1928. (*Source, Adrian Pingstone, Wikimedia Commons*)

by another monk from Llancarfan, named Lifris. We first meet this Arthur when he is with Cei (Kay) and Bedwyr (Bedivere), 'three valiant heroes', who together witness the abduction of the saint's future mother while sitting on a hilltop playing dice. Arthur lusts after the woman but is persuaded to pursue her attackers rather than her; thus the woman is able to conceive the saint, according to God's plan. But Lifris's Arthur is a petty tyrant who gets his just desserts. In the narrative, St Cadoc gives protection to a man who has killed three of Arthur's soldiers. Arthur demands a herd of cattle as compensation for the death of three of his men. Cadoc duly delivers the cattle as demanded, but Arthur obstinately refuses to accept any cattle except those of a certain colour. When cows of an acceptable hue are finally delivered, the saint duly turns them into bundles of ferns.

Slightly later than these texts is *De Gestis Regum Anglorum* (*Deeds of the Kings of the English*), written in around 1125 by the English historian William of Malmesbury. William lamented the 'nonsense' written about Arthur, who 'plainly deserves to be the subject of truthful history rather than false fables,' and maintains that Arthur was a vital figure in English history who,

> long sustained his sinking country, and roused the broken courage of its citizens for war; afterwards, in the siege of Mount Badon, spurred on by the image of the Mother of our Lord, which he habitually bore in his arms, he slew nine hundred of the enemy by his own hand in an incredible slaughter.

William is also one of the first historians to set down the presumption that Arthur has no known grave but will rise again – a belief that had apparently become rooted firmly in the hearts of the people of Cornwall. (According to an account by Herman of Laon, written in around 1146 and entitled *Concerning the Miracles of Saint Maria of Laon*, a riot erupted in the market town of Bodmin in 1113 when one of Herman's fellow monks had the boldness to deny publicly the possibility of Arthur's rebirth. The monks from Laon in Northeast France were in Cornwall as part of a journey through Southwest England raising funds to rebuild their church after it had been destroyed by fire in the previous year; it seems that the argument in Bodmin broke out when the group was approached by a local man seeking a cure for his withered arm.)

Geoffrey of Monmouth's King Arthur

The greatest single contribution – ever – to the propagation of the legend of King Arthur was made in the second quarter of the twelfth century by a historian named Geoffrey of Monmouth. Geoffrey's work inspired generations of later writers who plundered it extensively for source material, and his version of the stories has informed the popular understanding of Arthur into the present day. Yet despite Geoffrey bringing King Arthur to a wide audience during the high Middle Ages, little is known of him.

Geoffrey was probably born in around the year 1100 in Monmouth, a small town at the meeting point of the rivers Wye and Monnow, which mark the southern stretches of the border between England and Wales. Today Monmouth is situated along the short reach of the Wye that flows entirely through Wales, though throughout its history it has been disputed territory, with frequent spats over whether it is in fact an English or a Welsh town. During the time of William the Conqueror this was a rebellious border region, and Geoffrey is thought to have been the scion of Breton lords whom William settled hereabouts in the 1090s to put a lid on any trouble that might brew amid the solemn hills of the Black Mountains or the dense woodlands of the Forest of Dean, in the midst of which Monmouth lies. Geoffrey's contemporaries knew him as Galfridus Arturus (Geoffrey Arthur), a reference either to his scholarly interest in King Arthur, or to the name of his father; he appears to have been a career cleric, serving as a canon in the Oxford area, possibly at the secular college of St George's, which was attached to the chapel at Oxford Castle and was founded just eight years after the Norman invasion. The college was not part of Oxford University, for at this time there was no formal university here, but it was home to one of the informal groupings of students and 'masters' that formed the earliest incarnation of an academic community in the city. In 1152 Geoffrey left Oxford to take up an appointment as Bishop of St Asaph in North Wales – though continuous armed struggles in this querulous part of the country meant that he probably never visited his see. He seems to have died in either 1154 or 1155; some sources (or legends) maintain that he died in Llandaff in South Wales and was buried either there or at St Asaph.

By the time of Geoffrey's death his great work *Historia Regum Britanniae* (*History of the Kings of Britain*) was widely popular. It has probably first

Title page of a 1508 edition of Geoffrey of Monmouth's *History of the Kings of Britain*. (*Source, Wikimedia Commons*)

appeared around 1135, though was not his first book; that was *Prophesies of Merlin*, which was incorporated into the *Historia* as Book VII. Blending history, romance, literary imagination and legend into a seamless whole, the *Historia* was quite unlike any work that had gone before, and must have caused something of a minor sensation on its completion. Yet like many other works concerning King Arthur, the *Historia* is a product of the times in which it was written – and Geoffrey was working on the *Historia* during some very troubled times, as in 1135 England was plunged into a political crisis concerning the royal succession. In that year Henry I, a son of William the Conqueror, died without a clear heir; although Henry had chosen his nephew Stephen of Blois to be his successor, many championed Henry's daughter Matilda as the rightful monarch, and the resultant civil war that broke out was to blight King Stephen's shaky twenty-year reign. A place of refuge was needed for England's literate classes during this time of national crisis, and Geoffrey's tales of the heroic deeds of kings gone by fitted the bill perfectly. His book opens with the purported settlement of Britain by the warrior-king Brutus (or Brute of Troy), an almost certainly mythical figure who was supposedly the grandson of the Trojan hero Aeneas. Thereafter it follows Britain's fortunes up until the death of Cadwalladr, King of Gwynedd, who died around 680. Along the way Geoffrey's narrative takes in Julius Caesar's invasions of Britain, two kings (out of a total of 114) that were later immortalised by William Shakespeare, namely Lear and Cymbeline – and the deeds and life of King Arthur, which take up around a third of the narrative.

Geoffrey claimed in the book's dedication that the source for his material was an 'ancient book ... that told in orderly fashion the deeds of all the kings of Britain'. This mysterious book had been written in the 'British tongue' (ancient Welsh or Breton) and, Geoffrey claimed, had been given to him by Walter, Archdeacon of Oxford, the provost of St George's College who died in 1151. Many modern historians have dismissed this claim. After all, the ploy of invoking a lost source when presenting a historical work was not new in the Middle Ages, for it allowed authors to make a claim to the veracity of their work when in reality much of it was made up (though it is possible that the Archdeacon furnished Geoffrey with some materials in the Welsh language that helped inspire his work). Geoffrey's other sources include the *Historia Brittonum*, along with the writings of Bede and Gildas (neither of whom mention King Arthur). Narratives and characters from these works were embellished by Geoffrey with material drawn from oral tradition and, most vitally of all, from his own imagination – and so the crucial question that occupies students of Arthuriana is exactly how much, and which parts, of the *Historia* were simply made up. Certainly, Geoffrey seems to have made use of the list of Arthur's twelve battles against the Saxons found in the *Historia Brittonum,* and he also mentions the battle of Camlann from the *Annales Cambriae.* Many of the names for Arthur's close family and companions are drawn from Welsh texts, as is the name of his mythical sword, Caliburnus (which later became Excalibur in subsequent Arthurian tales in the French language). While accepting that names and key events in the *Historia* might have been borrowed from tradition, the historian Brynley Roberts has argued that 'the Arthurian section is Geoffrey's literary creation, and it owes nothing to prior narrative'. His words echo those of a much earlier scholar, William of Newburgh, who a few decades after the work was completed sneered that Geoffrey had taken 'the ancient fictions of the Britons and added his own to them ... cloaking [events] in the honest name of history'. The consensus among most historians is that while the style of Geoffrey's work might have conveyed the illusion of an authoritative narrative, which stood up to comparison with passages in the Old Testament and classical works such as the *Aeneid*, it was in fact a hoax, designed to be uplifting and entertaining – but not a work of historical record.

However much Geoffrey's work was one of imagination, he had changed Arthur forever. No longer was Arthur the blood-soaked warrior of the darkest part of the Dark Ages; instead, Geoffrey of Monmouth's Arthur was 'a youth of unparalleled courage and generosity' when he was crowned king at the age of just 15 – a courage that was 'joined with that sweetness of temper and innate goodness as gained him universal love'. According to Geoffrey's narrative, Arthur was the greatest of British rulers. Yet his deeds were placed in an apparently historical sixth-century Britain that was expressed in a detail and manner that made them relevant to Geoffrey's twelfth-century audience (the country over which Arthur presided was, for instance, easily recognisable as the centralised feudal state that was twelfth-century England; for example, Arthur spends Christmas at York and appoints a new archbishop there, just as William the Conqueror had done). Given all this, it is not surprising that Geoffrey of Monmouth's King Arthur became central to the literary imagination of the later Middle Ages. Geoffrey had provided Britons with a new national epic in the manner of the *Aeneid*, and a new Emperor-hero in the manner of Beowulf, Alexander the Great or Charlemagne – while the character of Merlin and the details concerning the final fate of Arthur, so pivotal in the 'romances' that were to follow, owe their origins directly to him.

French Chroniclers of Arthur: Chrétien de Troyes and the Vulgate Cycle

Geoffrey of Monmouth's work was particularly well received in Normandy and Brittany, which at that time were independent kingdoms, yet to be swallowed up into France. Links between what is now northwest France and southwest England ran deep. During the time of the Saxon incursions many Celts had fled across the Channel to Brittany, whose name – bestowed on the region by later missionaries from Ireland and Britain – means 'Little Britain'. But when Geoffrey wrote his *Historia*, the flow of people and influence was in the opposite direction. In the twelfth century much of England was ruled by French-speaking noble families who owed their powerful positions to William the Conqueror and his victory at Hastings. In 1154, around the time that Geoffrey died, William's great-grandson Henry II acceded to the throne of England, and he not only had a French father, Geoffrey Plantagenet, the Count of Anjou and Maine, but also a French wife, Eleanor, Duchess of Aquitaine. French language, art and architectural styles began to dominate in England, in everything from the building of cathedrals to the illumination of manuscripts to the legal system – and at the same time the stories of Arthur became popular in France. A chronicler named William, chaplain to the Bishop of Léon in southwest Brittany, wove a celebration of Arthur into his *Legend of Saint Goeznovius,* while wandering minstrels told stores of Arthur to audiences in towns and villages. Soon a number of places in Brittany had become inalienably linked to Arthurian legends. Tristan and

The Centre de L'imaginaire Arthurien near Rennes. (*Source, Wikimedia commons*)

Iseult were supposed to have hidden in Trémazan Castle on the rocky coast of Finistère, while the Paimpont Forest west of Rennes was home to the sorceress Morgan le Fay and to Merlin, who was imprisoned by the enchantress Viviane in a remote spot now known as 'Merlin's Stone'. This ancient forest was said to be the Brocéliande Forest of the Arthurian Romances, and to this day a lakeside chateau at Concoret near the forest is home to the Centre de l'Imaginaire Arthurien, the geographical epicentre of Arthurian traditions in France, which offers everything from guided tours of the forest with costumed storytellers, to children's workshops, exhibitions, knights-of-yore spectacles and a specialist bookshop for Arthuriana browsing.

The first translation of Geoffrey's work into Norman French is believed to have been made by Geoffrey Gaimar, of whom little is known; shortly afterwards, in around 1155, a much more widely distributed translation was made by Maistre Wace, an Anglo-Norman poet who was one of Henry II's courtiers. More is known of Wace than of Gaimar. He was born on the island of Jersey in around 1100, completed his education in Caen, and visited southern England at least once during his life. Wace gave his work – which consisted of 15,000 lines of French verse – the title *Roman de Brut*, after Brutus of Troy, whom Geoffrey had named as the founder of Britain. And he did more than simply translate Geoffrey's work. He treated the source material with considerable freedom, using direct speech to give his work a dramatic and emotional heft that Geoffrey's rather dry prose somewhat lacked. And Wace also made one vital and lasting contribution to the great canon of Arthurian myth: he was the first writer to suggest that Arthur and his knights held their discussions around the Round Table.

The translation made by Wace soon passed into the hands of an even more widely read poet and chronicler, Chrétien de Troyes. As his name suggests, Chrétien probably hailed from Troyes, a city on the River Seine southeast of Paris; his most productive period of writing was the 1170s and 1180s, when he was active in the court of Marie, Countess of Champagne, a daughter of the redoubtable Eleanor of Aquitaine. Under Marie's patronage Chrétien wrote a number of epic poems based on Arthurian, French and classical stories. But he presents us with a very different Arthur to that of Geoffrey of Monmouth. Instead of a great and ferocious warrior, who laughs as he personally slaughters witches and giants, the Arthur of Chrétien frequently assumes a wise and dignified demeanour,

Chrétien de Troyes depicted in an engraving of 1530. (*Source, Bibliothèque Nationale de France, Wikimedia Commons*)

with an aura about him that is both remote and majestic. And rather than concerning himself with mundane matters, Chrétien's Arthur adopts a rather lofty, glacial personality – and, moreover, he is side-lined in favour of the deeds of other characters, most notably the various knights of the

Round Table. Another departure from Geoffrey's work is Chrétien's use of dramatic tension in his narrative, contrasting the companionship of the court against the loneliness of the quests undertaken by the various knights; the inner psychological stress of the characters gives these romances a dramatic power that resonates in a way that previous versions of these tales do not. Part of this dramatic tension comes from the code of carefully restrained 'courtly' love that Chrétien's characters abide by. This notion was first utilised in the Arthur stories by Maistre Wace, but it was Chrétien who championed it in his story of Lancelot and Guinevere. A tradition emanating from Southern France, 'courtly love' invests noble women with an aura of near-divinity, and instils a sense of duty and obedience in their pursuers. Indeed the whole notion of courtly love lay at the heart of a 'romance', a story that placed a great emphasis on a knight's courtly and unfulfilled love for a lady, often the wife of a lord or his feudal superior. At the same time the knight adopts a recognised code of chivalry when dealing with his enemies and his fellow knights.

Chrétien was one of the last French chroniclers of Arthur who told their stories exclusively in poetry. From around 1210 onwards the tales began to be told in prose, and the most significant of these 'romances' – which to a medieval audience were the same as a novel to today's readers – was the so-called Vulgate Cycle, a series of five Middle French prose works written in the first half of the thirteenth century. King Arthur is the central figure who unites these tales, which comprise stories of Merlin, Sir Galahad's quest for the Holy Grail, the death of Arthur and the subsequent collapse of his kingdom, and the story of how Joseph of Arimathea brings the Holy Grail to Britain. The cycle continues the trend towards reducing the role played by Arthur in the legends, partly through characters such as Galahad and Merlin playing prominent parts. The tales present, too, a fully expressed moral universe, in which Arthur stands for royalty and leadership, Lancelot for human achievement through chivalry, Galahad for pure perfection, Perceval for redemption through innocent faith, and Bors for good works by which he expiates his one venal sin. The cycle also makes Mordred the result of an incestuous relationship between Arthur and his sister Morgause, and establishes the role of Camelot, first mentioned in passing by Chrétien de Troyes in his *Lancelot*, as Arthur's primary court.

This series of texts was quickly followed by the Post-Vulgate Cycle, written in the 1230s and often focusing on the quest for the Holy Grail. Contemporaneous with these texts are similar epics written in German,

The Porta della Pescheria of Modena Cathedral, which depicts Arthurian scenes around the arch. (*Source, Wikimedia Commons*)

whose authors include Wolfram, a Bavarian knight of whom little is known, whose tale tells of the story of Parzival and the Holy Grail, and Gottfried von Strassburg, whose subject was Tristan. These and other works comprise immense and often unwieldy fantasies that tell of endless combats, prolonged quests and the rescue of successive damsels in distress. Although Arthur's role is side-lined even more in these texts, their popularity meant that by the end of the thirteenth century the king had become a familiar figure in European myth, folklore and tradition. His story even reached as far as Italy, where it was spread by bards accompanying Norman and Breton knights campaigning there; indeed, the earliest representation of Arthur in art is in a scene carved into the archivolt of a great doorway, the Porta della Pescheria, in the cathedral at Modena, near Bologna. Dating from the early twelfth century, the scene, which curves around the doorway with an inscription above, depicts King Arthur (Artus de Bretania) with his supporters attempting the rescue of Guinevere from a castle defended by Burmaltus – a story initially told by Caradoc of Llancarfan in his *Life of Gildas* and developed by Chrétien de Troyes in his *Prose Lancelot*.

Even as the stories of King Arthur were being told and retold in continental Europe, new versions were still appearing in England. In around 1400 an anonymous poet wrote the alliterative poem *Morte Arthure*, in which many of Arthur's exploits mirror and celebrate those of the Plantagenet kings – most notably in the case of Arthur's battle against the Roman Emperor Lucius Hiberius, which closely resembles Edward III's famous victory at Crécy in 1346. The work was written in an ancient form of English verse where the need for an alliterative vocabulary resulted in the use of a rich text full of obscure words and resonant phrases, drawing on Anglo Saxon and Norse. Instead of the end of each line rhyming, the style of the poem dictated that most words in each line begun with the same sound – a literary form for recital at feasts rather than for private reading. The form reached its flowering in *Sir Gawain and the Green Knight*, written some time between 1360 and 1390 by – again – an anonymous author, and considered the outstanding achievement of medieval Arthurian writing.

Thomas Malory and the Morte d'Arthur

The culmination of these narratives was *Le Morte d'Arthur*, the comprehensive and authoritative retelling of the Arthurian legends written by an English writer named Thomas Malory in the late fifteenth century. Scholars have been exercised to a considerable extent by a debate as to who Thomas Malory actually was. Four knights with this name were active in late fifteenth-century England and all are possible candidates, but the consensus seems to be that the real author of *Morte d'Arthur* was the Thomas Malory who was a Warwickshire knight, a member of parliament and a landowner – and a notorious criminal.

This particular Malory was born in around 1410, to a family whose estates centred on the village of Newbold Revel, which lies a few miles northwest of Rugby. A colourful and contradictory figure, Malory was accused on various occasions of extortion, theft, kidnap and rape, and was for a time imprisoned in Maxstoke Castle near Warwick, a place of incarceration from which he escaped by daringly swimming across the moat. Malory's crimes seem to have been committed as part of a long-standing feud between his patrons, the Earls of Warwick, and a neighbouring landowner, the Duke of Buckingham. In 1462, during the violence and chaos of the Wars of the Roses, he accompanied the Earl of Warwick (the famous 'Warwick the Kingmaker') and the Yorkist King Edward IV on their expedition to Northumberland, and was present at the sieges of Bamburgh and Alnwick castles (to which reference is made in *Morte d'Arthur*). When Warwick broke with Edward after a perceived slight and joined the Lancastrian side, Malory followed him, and in 1468 he became embroiled in a plot to overthrow Edward IV, for which he was imprisoned in London's notorious Newgate prison. It is thought that it was here, during the last two years of his life, that he wrote *Le Morte d'Arthur*. As a prisoner of some social standing, Malory would have had access to the library of a monastery that adjoined the prison, where he could consult existing texts that told the story of King Arthur and his knights (his work drew extensively from the Vulgate Cycle). He died on 14 March 1471 and was buried in Greyfriars Church on Newgate Street, close to the prison (this church was destroyed in the Great Fire of London, and Wren's replacement church was destroyed in the Blitz; Malory's tomb has long vanished – but the shell of Wren's church now forms a park where City workers can eat their lunch). So Malory the writer seems to be a very different person to Malory the habitual criminal – but some have suggested that the many charges against him were fabricated by powerful supporters of the House of Lancaster, and thus there is no problem in reconciling the high sentiments of the author's own life with the magnificent work of literature he produced.

Greyfriars Newgate Street in the City of London, the now-ruined church where Thomas Malory was probably buried. (*Source, John Salmon, Wikimedia Commons*)

Le Morte d'Arthur was the last great literary work written in England before the introduction of printing, and it is also the earliest great work written in English for which we are dependent fully on a printed (rather than handwritten) text. The printed edition of *Morte d'Arthur* was published in

1485, fourteen years after Malory's death, by William Caxton, who was the book's editor, printer and publisher. It was Caxton who divided the work into sections, and who provided the summaries at the start of each chapter. Many scholars have pointed out the carelessness of Caxton's print-setting and editing, identifying passages where it is impossible to believe that Malory's intentions were the same as that which is presented to us in Caxton's printed edition. But all subsequent editions, including those available today, are derived from Caxton's original version, though through the ages obsolete words have been replaced and, in the nineteenth century, the violence of some of the passages was softened, lest the tales be read by impressionable schoolboys. Nonetheless, it is the *Morte d'Arthur* that has informed our awareness and appreciation of Arthur and his milieu from the fifteenth century until the present day; even in the early twenty-first century every book, film and computer game that derives its inspiration from the Arthurian legends owes something to Thomas Malory.

Malory's work, which was written in English, is divided into eight books. Five of these recount the deeds of Arthur's knights, following the exploits of Lancelot, Galahad and Tristan (known as Sir Tristram de Lyones in Malory's work) and their quest for the Holy Grail. The other three books tell the story of Arthur, and include such iconic episodes as the sword in the stone, which was Malory's enduring contribution to Arthuriana (in much the same way as his predecessor Maistre Wace had given the world the legend of the Round Table). To what extent Malory originally intended each book (or combination of books) to be independent, stand-alone tales is a matter of debate. Was his intention from the start to produce a complete cycle of stories, or did he simply make progress by adding more tales to his original work until he reached a point where attempts at completeness were almost inevitable? The French Vulgate Cycle was, at the time of the work's composition, the most complete version of the tales of Arthur and his knights. But that cycle was vast and unwieldy and a number of attempts had already been made to reduce it into a coherent whole in both France and Germany; when it first appeared, Malory's version was clearly the undisputed masterpiece that embraced the whole story of Arthur and his knights in an easily digestible fashion. Nonetheless, his principal source was still the Vulgate Cycle, rather than Geoffrey of Monmouth – as Caxton himself wrote in his preface, 'Sir Thomas Malorye did take [his sources from] certain books of French, and reduced [these] into English'.

In many ways it is the first two books of *Morte d'Arthur* that are the most iconic in the evolution of the King Arthur myth. They concentrate on the life of Arthur, beginning with his birth to Uther Pendragon and Igraine (which largely follows the account of Geoffrey of Monmouth, in which Merlin disguises Uther as Igraine's husband Gorlois so that Uther can sleep with her), and then his childhood, which is spent in the idyllic country home of Arthur's foster father, a knight named Sir Ector. Next comes Arthur's elevation to the kingship of a leaderless England when he extracts the fabled sword from the stone. This scene was set by Malory in a London churchyard, and in an authorial aside he complains to his readers that the French source from which he took this part of the story doesn't specify which church it was. He seems to suggest it was St Paul's Cathedral – though it is doubtful whether a church by this name stood on this spot during the putative time of King Arthur. Nevertheless,

> In the midst thereof was an anvil of steel a foot on high, and therein stuck a fair sword naked by the point, and letters there were written in gold about the sword that said thus; 'who so pulleth out this sword of this stone and anvil is rightwise king born of all England'.

The rest of the story is one of the most familiar narratives ever told; the best modern version occurs at the end of T.H. White's 1958 novel *The Sword in the Stone*, in which the boy Arthur innocently announces that he 'found [the sword] stuck in a stone, outside a church', and afterwards becomes so overwhelmed with his new role as king that he wishes he 'had never seen that filthy sword at all', and bursts into tears at seeing his brother and father kneeling before him. As to the preceding events, Malory tells us that many knights attempt to pull the sword out from its stone prison, but fail; Arthur alone succeeds, though no one else is present when he draws the sword for the first time, as all the other knights are taking part in a New Year's Day joust. He takes the gleaming prize to his brother Kay (Sir Ector's son), who has charged him with looking after his horses and weaponry. Kay then takes it to his father, Sir Ector, claiming he – not Arthur – has drawn it from the stone. Sir Ector, suspicious of Kay's claims, makes both boys pull the sword from the stone again, in front of him; Kay duly fails, but 'Arthur … pulled it out easily. And therewithal Sir Ector knelt down to the earth, and Sir Kay. "Alas," said

The boy Arthur pulling the sword from the stone, as depicted in one of the windows of the Halls of Chivalry in Tintagel. (*Andrew Beattie*)

Arthur, "my own dear father and brother, why kneel ye to me?" Ector's reply contains a revelation concerning the nature of Arthur's birth and upbringing; 'Nay, nay, my lord Arthur, it is not so; I was never your father nor of your blood … And then Sir Ector told him all, how he was betaken him for to nourish him, and by whose commandment, and by Merlin's deliverance.' Arthur then draws the sword from the stone a third time, in front of assembled Lords and Commons – a sure sign of the updating of the story that Malory undertook, for the two houses of parliament had only been in existence for two centuries when he wrote it, and nothing like these bodies would have existed during the time of King Arthur. Notwithstanding this, parliament duly declares Arthur to be King of England, and the young man immediately embarks on a series of military campaigns around the country against his enemies. Everywhere he meets with success, spurred by his military prowess and by the wise counsel of Merlin. He also conceives a son, Mordred, by his half-sister, Morgause, though at the time Arthur is unaware of her relationship to him. When Arthur discovers the terrible truth he takes Merlin's advice and sends every newborn boy in his kingdom out to sea in a boat, an event that echoes King Herod's slaughtering of the innocents in the New Testament. In the event the boat is wrecked and all but one of the boys perish; the survivor is Mordred, who later on becomes Arthur's nemesis and slayer.

In previous Arthurian narratives Arthur had gained the crown of England in a much more prosaic way. Maistre Wace recorded how 'the bishops sent word to each other and the barons assembled; they summoned Arthur, Uther's son, and crowned him at Silchester.' But later on divine oversight began to creep into the picture, reflecting tensions between crown and baronage in England and the concern that inheritance, the simple passing of a crown from father to son, might not after all be the best way of arranging succession. Might the country be better off if the successor to a king was worthy, rather than just next in line? It was concerns such as these that exercised the barons who quarrelled with King John and drew up the Magna Carta, and which informed the early development of the story of the sword-in-the-stone; for although Malory popularised and embellished the story, he did not pluck it from his imagination. The French source he mentions was probably a work entitled *Merlin*, whose composition is attributed to the French writer Robert de Boron (though might have been the work of a continuator, who finished the story around the year 1200 following Robert de Boron's death). In this work the story of Arthur pulling the sword from the stone is dealt with briefly, leaving Malory to flesh it out into something iconic nearly three centuries later. Yet even this seemingly original French version may have been based on much earlier sources and stories. King-making rituals involving large stones abounded in the Celtic world. At Dunadd, an Iron Age hilltop fort in southwest Scotland, there is a large footprint imprinted in a stone that might have played a part in initiation or coronation rituals of kings. Then there is the legend of an obscure Italian saint, Galgano, who died at Montesiepi near Siena in 1181 and whose cult was championed by monks of the Cistercian order. A sword lodged in a rock was an important feature of his story, and features as a motif on the curly top end of the crozier carried by Archbishops of Siena in the late Middle Ages. Such tales of a mystical sword set fast into a stone might have spread north to France via monks travelling from monastery to monastery. Still other scholars have suggested that the story has its origins in antiquity. In the fourth century the Roman historian Ammianus Marcellinus wrote of the 'savage custom' of a people known as the Alans who lived between the Black Sea and the Caspian Sea, whose custom it was 'to stick a naked sword in the earth and worship it as the god of war'. However, the Arthurian story involves the sword being drawn from its stone, rather than, as it does in these sources, representing the god of war and ritualistic blood sacrifice. But in the origin story of the Scythian people, who lived in a vast area stretching from modern-day Ukraine to Tajikistan, there is another strange echo of the sword in the stone legend. Their founding myth details how four golden objects one day fell to earth, and the youngest son of a prominent family was the only one who was able to pick them up; when his older brothers tried, they found the gold too hot to touch. So the younger brother becomes the king, and the possession of these sacred objects legitimises his descendants. Could this story have reached Europe via members of these tribes serving in the Roman army, and then have been twisted so that a sword is the object of mystical providence, rather than gold objects falling from the sky? Such questions have caused considerable debate among scholars analysing Malory's tale.

Following the account of Arthur gaining his crown by drawing the sword from the stone, the first book of *Morte d'Arthur* tells of Arthur's marriage to Guinevere, his inheritance of the Round Table from her father Leodegrance, and the gathering of his loyal knights around it at Camelot. The second book draws heavily in narrative and subject matter from the alliterative poem *Morte Arthure*, and covers Arthur's military campaign against the Roman Empire. This begins when envoys arrive on British shores from Emperor Lucius (who ruled in the second century AD – much earlier than the reign of any 'historical' Arthur). They accuse Arthur of refusing to pay tribute to Rome, 'contrary to the statutes and decrees made by the noble and worthy Julius Caesar'. Spoiling for a fight, Arthur turns the tables on the envoys, demanding tribute from Lucius and evoking the names of Belinus the Great and Sir Bryne, the mythical British conquerors of Rome. Leaving his court in the hands of Sir Constantine of Cornwall, Arthur sails to Normandy where he joins forces with his cousin Hoel and kills a giant that is terrorising the people from its lair in the holy island of Mont St Michel. Subsequently Arthur defeats Lucius in battle – Malory modelled Arthur's campaign in France on that of Henry V's in the weeks leading up to the Battle of Agincourt – and is crowned Roman Emperor by the Pope.

The final book in *Le Morte d'Arthur* concerns the death of Arthur. After Mordred reveals Guinevere's adulterous relationship with Lancelot, Arthur is forced to sentence Guinevere to burn at the stake. While the terrible execution is underway he orders that the scene be guarded so that any rescue attempt from Lancelot, who has fled Camelot, can be repulsed. But the knights who have been appointed to guard Guinevere refuse to arm themselves, and when Lancelot's party launches a raid on the execution site, many of them are killed, though they do not save Guinevere. Enraged at her death, Lancelot fights Arthur in a series of battles waged across northern England and France. During one of his campaigns against Lancelot in France, Arthur receives a message that Mordred has usurped his throne, so he leads his forces back across the English Channel for a final, decisive battle with Mordred, which is fought at a place named as Camlann. At the close of the battle Arthur leads a charge against Mordred and impales him with a spear – but with the last few ounces of his strength Mordred impales himself even further, bringing him within striking distance of Arthur, and delivers a devastating blow to Arthur's head with his sword. As Arthur lies wounded, a barge carrying ladies clad in black hoods emerges from the shadows; one of the ladies is the enchantress Morgan le Fay, Arthur's half-sister. In a magical close to the tale they take Arthur onto the boat and depart for the mystical Isle of Avalon – the king's eventual fate never to be revealed.

So did King Arthur ever actually exist?

The historical basis for the King Arthur legend has long been debated by scholars. One school of thought, citing entries in the

Historia Brittonum and *Annales Cambriae*, sees Arthur as a genuine historical figure, a Romano-British leader who fought against the invading Anglo-Saxons some time in the late fifth to early sixth century. But those who make the claim for Arthur being a genuine figure from history face a major problem when they cite these texts as support – for they were written down three centuries (or more) after Arthur's supposed rule. This fact, together with the lack of any other convincing early evidence from archaeological sources, is the reason many contemporary historians exclude Arthur from their accounts of sub-Roman Britain. In the view of the academic Thomas Charles-Edwards, a former Oxford Professor of Celtic and a noted historian of the Dark Ages, 'at this stage of the enquiry, one can only say that there may well have been an historical Arthur [but ...] the historian can as yet say nothing of value about him'. His view is echoed by Edward James in his book *Britain in the First Millennium*. 'It has been quite common for historians to subscribe to the "no smoke without fire" theory of Arthur,' he writes, 'even though the smoke is very thin, and indistinguishable from highland mist'.

The debate is centuries old. William Caxton, Thomas Malory's editor, publisher and printer, was a proponent of the Arthur-was-real school of thought, but was well aware of the opposing arguments. In his preface to *Morte d'Arthur* he explained that 'diverse men hold opinion that there was no such Arthur,' adding that 'some chronicles make of him no mention, nor remember him nothing, nor of his knights.' But he then goes on to discuss the arguments put forward by those who believe Arthur to have existed, mentioning that it was possible to see his tomb in Glastonbury, the skull of Sir Gawain at Dover Castle, and the Round Table itself at Winchester. In the end Caxton concluded that, 'Then all these things considered, there can no man reasonably gainsay but there was a king of this land named Arthur.' But maybe his views are not really all that surprising; after all, he was a publisher with a book to sell.

There have always been historians who are believers in the veracity of a historical Arthur. An early one was John Leland, Henry VIII's chief topographer and antiquary, who argued for Arthur's genuineness in his 1544 book *Assertion of Arthur*. Three and a half centuries later, in 1893, Heinrich Zimmer, a German historian who at the time was considered the world's leading scholar of the Celtic age, published a study of the *Historia Brittonum* that accepted the real possibility that Arthur might have lived. His work provided the trigger for a succession of scholars who accepted that Arthur was real. In 1923 the American scholar James Douglas Bruce admitted that although the evidence was 'meagre, relatively late, and almost wholly fantastical', King Arthur should be accepted as 'real … a man of Romanised descent, or a Romanised Celt'. John Morris (1913–1977), formerly senior lecturer in ancient history at University College London, made the putative reign of Arthur the organising principle of *The Age of Arthur,* his 1973 study of Dark Age Britain and Ireland, which was the first attempt by a professional historian to build a picture of Britain during the period 350–650. Morris never doubts that King Arthur lived and ruled during this time. 'The personality of Arthur is unknown and unknowable,' he wrote. 'But he was as real as Alfred the Great or William the Conqueror; and his impact upon future ages mattered as much, or more.' Yet even he found little to say about a historical Arthur in his book, much of which concerns the general history of Celtic Britain (and Brittany) during that era. *The Age of Arthur* found a popular audience among the public but was regarded with derision by many academics, such as Guy Halsall, who commented that 'there are essentially two things that you need to know about Morris's *Age of Arthur*: one is that it is a marvellous, inspiring read; the other is that very little of it can be relied upon.' This trend continues today. Bookshop shelves still groan with titles claiming to 'reveal' the 'real' Arthur – or an aspect of his story, such as the 'true' site of Camelot or Avalon. According to Alan Lupack in his *Oxford Guide to Arthurian Literature and Legend* (2005) these books are the 'siren claims of pseudo-histories' – and there are lots and lots of them, as just a cursory glance at the titles listed on book-retailing websites relating to King Arthur will reveal. None are scholarly histories; instead they are entertainments, relying often on outlandish and occasionally baseless supposition or eccentric reading of ancient texts, their authors claiming that shining clues about the nature of Arthur lie within these texts when in reality the picture is as muddy as it's always been.

The nemesis of these historians are those who believe that Arthur never existed. The archaeologist Nowell Myres (1902–1989) complained that 'no figure on the borderline of history and mythology has wasted more of the historian's time', while the historian David Dumville, who has held posts in a number of British and American universities, maintained that,

> we can dispose of him [Arthur] quite briefly. He owes his
> place in our history books to a 'no smoke without fire'
> school of thought ...The fact of the matter is that there is no
> historical evidence about Arthur; we must reject him from
> our histories and, above all, from the titles of our books.

This view is an old one, stretching back to Polydore Vergil, a visiting
collector of papal taxes whom Henry VII commissioned to write a history
of England. In the resulting *Historia Anglia* of 1534, Vergil sneered that the
figure whom the people of England 'extol unto the heavens' never actually
existed – which earned a rebuke from John Leland, in which he accused
Vergil of being 'faint hearted, lukewarm and so negligent that he makes
me not only to laugh, but also to be angry' – and added, for good measure,
that the renowned scholar was 'filled with Italian bitterness'. In the mid-
nineteenth century the distinguished Anglo-Saxon scholar John Mitchell
Kemble dismissed Arthurian history as 'a confused mass of traditions
borrowed from the most heterogenous sources ... in which the smallest
possible amount of historical truth is involved in a great deal of fable.'
Adherents of this point of view argue that Arthur is absent from three vital
texts that inform our history of the Dark Ages – two of which have already
been mentioned in this book. These are *De Excidio et Conquestu Britanniae*
(*On the Ruin and Conquest of Britain*) by the sixth-century British cleric
Gildas, and the Venerable Bede's celebrated *Ecclesiastical History of the
English People*. The third is the *Anglo-Saxon Chronicle*, a collection of
annals and reports begun during the reign of Alfred the Great (871–899)
and periodically updated over the centuries that followed. Scholars who
doubt the existence of Arthur often claim that he was originally a fictional
hero of folklore – or even a half-forgotten Celtic deity – who later became
credited with real deeds of the distant past. In this way he shared the same
trajectory through myth and history as other legendary but less venerated
figures from the same era, such as the Kentish rulers Hengist and Horsa,
and their Saxon overlord Vortigern.

The last strand of this debate is one that blends the two sides of
the argument, and claims that the legend of Arthur has its genesis in
a historical figure with a similar name. One of the most widely-read
proponents of this school of thought is the popular historian Geoffrey
Ashe, who believes that Geoffrey of Monmouth's narrative is partially
derived from a lost source telling of the deeds of a fifth-century Breton

33

leader named Riothamus, who might have led British troops into Gaul in around 469. Could Geoffrey's Arthur have descended from memories of this war fought by a British king against German enemies deep inside Dark Age France? Historians have been reluctant to follow Ashe and similar writers in their convictions.

Tennyson and Wagner: Arthuriana in the nineteenth century

Malory's *Morte d'Arthur* represented the apogee of Arthurian literature. The greater scrutiny on the veracity of the past that came with the Renaissance robbed the character of Arthur of some of his power to enthral audiences. As a result he lost his place in history, and 1634 saw the last printing of Malory's *Le Morte d'Arthur* for nearly 200 years. The Arthurian legends were not entirely abandoned in the seventeenth century, but the stories were taken less seriously, and were often used simply as a prism though which to examine the politics of the day. For instance, Richard Blackmore's epics *Prince Arthur* (1695) and *King Arthur* (1697) feature Arthur as a cipher for the struggles of William III against James II. Only John Dryden's 1691 masque *King Arthur,* in which the stories were presented in a form akin to modern opera with music by Henry Purcell, harked back to earlier, more reverential treatments of the subject. During the century that followed, no new works featuring the king saw the light of day and fashion tended to favour the classical rather than the medieval in literature, music and art. The most popular Arthurian tale throughout this period seems to be that of Tom Thumb, which was told first through chapbooks and later through the political plays of Henry Fielding; although the action of these stories is clearly set in Arthurian Britain, the treatment is humorous and King Arthur appears as a primarily comedic version of his character from the Romances.

After the turn of the nineteenth century Arthur's literary fortunes underwent a sea-change. The impetus came from a burgeoning interest in medievalism and romanticism that once again made fashionable the chivalric ideals embodied in the 'Arthur of romance'. Suddenly the portrayal of heroic moments in British history were all the rage, with Sir Walter Scott tapping into the new appetite for olden-days escapism in a series of historical novels, beginning with *Waverley* in 1814. Ten years earlier he had edited a new version of the legend of Tristram and Iseult, and in 1816, Malory's *Le Morte d'Arthur* was reprinted for the first time since 1634 – in three editions. But it was poets, rather than novelists, who capitalised most successfully on the public's appetite for all things Arthurian. In 1832 Alfred, Lord Tennyson, published his first Arthurian poem *The Lady of Shalott*, which was eventually incorporated into his epic work the *Idylls of the King*, in which he reworked the entire narrative of Arthur's life for the Victorian era. On its first publication in 1859 the *Idylls* sold 10,000 copies within the first week; buoyed by its success, Tennyson was to reshape the work continuously for forty years, and the final version of the cycle did not appear until 1885. The poem, which draws its inspiration primarily from Malory, is set at intervals throughout the natural year; the segment *The Coming of Arthur* takes place on New Year's Day, for instance, while Arthur is married 'when the world is white with May', and the Grail appears at Camelot on a Summer's night. The final battle, in which Lancelot and Guinevere repent for their adultery and Arthur forgives them, takes place during the frozen depths of midwinter. The poem's keystone is the knightly fellowship of the Round Table, in which Arthur's knights are required,

> to reverence the king, as if he were / Their conscience, and their conscience as their King … To speak no slander, no, nor listen to it / To honour his own word as if his God's / To lead sweet lives in purest chastity / To love one maiden only, cleave to her / And worship her by years of noble deeds/ Until they won her.

Tennyson's works prompted a large number of imitators and generated considerable public interest in the legends of Arthur, which brought Malory's tales to a wider audience; the first version of *Le Morte d'Arthur* written in accessible, contemporary form was published in 1862, shortly after the *Idylls* appeared. The exploits of Tom Thumb were also given a makeover during the nineteenth century, his story now including more elements from the Arthurian romances.

Tennyson's great work inspired an enthusiasm for Arthur among the artists of the Pre-Raphaelite school, who looked for inspiration to the period before the Renaissance, and particularly to the time before the Italian painter Raphael – hence their name. In 1852 William Dyce carved Arthurian scenes on the wooden panelling of the monarch's robing room in the Houses of Parliament, and later on in the same decade Dante Gabriel Rossetti and his friends undertook a major cycle of frescoes based on Arthurian themes for the Oxford Union. Many of the works undertaken by these artists were, in effect, illustrations, as a thorough knowledge of the literary text is needed if the narrative provided by the picture is to be fully appreciated. Some Pre-Raphaelite artists also turned their hands to poetry, including William Morris, who published a collection of Arthurian poems in 1858 and founded a chivalric order with the painter Sir Edward Burne Jones; they once instructed a friend to learn Tennyson's *Sir Galahad* by heart before joining it. Morris's poems were inspired by Tennyson but shimmered with poignant, strong emotions and powerful visual images – such as when Guinevere is distracted at Mass by 'Lancelot's red-gold hair [which] would play, instead of sunlight, on the painted wall [and] mingled with dreams of what the priest did say'.

The revived interest in Arthurian romances also spread across the Atlantic to the United States. Books such as Sidney Lanier's The *Boy's King Arthur* (1880) reached a wide audience and provided inspiration for Mark Twain's *A Connecticut Yankee in King Arthur's Court* (1889), in which the great satirist poked fun at the vogue for Arthuriana. Twain's plot involves a hero named Hank who transforms from an amiable youth into a resolute dictator, and who uses his knowledge of science to enable him to create and then destroy a modern civilisation that has somehow developed in a medieval setting. In Germany Richard Wagner composed a cycle of Arthurian operas, from *Tristan und Isolde* (1859) to *Parsifal* (1882), which depicted Arthur's knights as a brotherhood – and an Aryan brotherhood too, lending the opera a decidedly sinister touch when seen through today's eyes. Arthur was also celebrated in France, where his exploits attracted writers just as fervently as it had six centuries previously when the Vulgate Cycle of stories was recited before kings and potentates. Edgar Quinet's long novel *Merlin L'Enchanteur* was a conscious attempt to present the legendary wizard as the anti-Christ, and featured Satan fathering Merlin by the nun Seraphina – though in the end Satan converts, destroying his own kingdom before kneeling in repentance in front of Merlin. Quinet presented Paris as the centre of Arthur's court and clearly wanted to create a great French national legend around the figure of Merlin. More successful was the symphonic poem *Viviane* by the composer Ernest Chausson, which tells the story of Merlin's love for Viviane, and which

Ludwig and Malwine Schnorr von Carolsfeld in the title roles of the original production of Richard Wagner's *Tristan and Isolde* in 1865. (*Source, Wikimedia Commons*)

was followed by *Le Roi Arthus*, which was first performed in Brussels in 1903 to largely enthusiastic notices, though many complained the music was a pale shadow of Wagner.

King Arthur in the twentieth century

Since 1900 the 'Arthur' industry has flourished like never before. King Arthur has been the subject of countless novels, dramas and films, while this book represents another aspect of Arthuriana, for publishers produce so many factual histories and anthologies relating to the king that even the most dedicated enthusiast is at risk of drowning in the printed word. In terms of literature, the opening decades of the twentieth century saw a sudden spike of interest in Arthur among dramatists, with plays such as Arthur Symons's *Tristan and Iseult*, Laurence Binyon's *Arthur; a Tragedy*, and Thomas Hardy's *The Famous Tragedy of the Queen of Cornwall*. In Germany, Eduard Stucken's cycle of Arthurian plays enjoyed considerable success when they were produced by Max Reinhardt at the Deutsches Theater in Berlin. In France, Jean Cocteau played with Arthurian themes in his *Les Chevaliers de la Table Ronde* (1937), in which Ginifer, a devil enslaved by the evil enchanter Merlin, impersonates Gawain, Guinevere and Galahad in turn. Cocteau's play abounds in theatrical flourishes, with a single actress playing the characters of Guinevere, Ginifer impersonating Guinevere, and Guinevere reincarnated in her daughter Blandine.

Poets were also busy, as they have been since the Dark Ages when it comes to retelling the exploits of Arthur. Between 1917 and 1927 the Pulitzer prize-winning poet Edwin Arlington Robinson wrote three long Arthurian poems that looked at the relevance of the myth to the modern world. *Merlin* examined the theme of the tension between the pursuit of private fulfilment and public duty during a time of crisis, and emphasised the psychology of character rather than events through powerful visual images. It was followed by *Lancelot* and then *Tristram*. In *A Midsummer Night and Other Tales* the poet laureate John Masefield presents the life of Arthur in a series of historical ballads while, in a wholly different vein, T.S. Eliot was heavily influenced by Arthurian legends in his composition of his modernist poem *The Waste Land* (1922). In this poem Eliot was particularly drawn to Jessie L. Weston's notion that the lance and cup of the grail procession (as first described by Chrétien de Troyes) were sexual symbols from the ancient past that were linked to equally ancient lore through figures on tarot cards. During the Second World War and its aftermath Arthur was reinvented once more, this time as a legendary resistance fighter who held out against Germanic invaders. In 1942 a series of radio plays by Clemence Dane, *The Saviours*, struck a particular chord in Britain by using a historical Arthur to embody the spirit of heroic resistance against desperate odds, while R.C. Sherriff's play *The Long Sunset* (1955) also saw Arthur rallying Romano–British resistance against invaders from across the North Sea.

In the years before and after the Second World War it was the novelist T.H. White that most shaped the figure of Arthur in the popular imagination. White wrote his first Arthurian novel, *The Sword in the Stone*, in the winter of 1937–8 'as a preface to Malory', and later wrote that the book 'was a kind of wish-fulfilment of the things I should like to have happened to me when I was a boy'. The novel focuses on the young boy, Wart – pronounced to rhyme with 'cart', we are told – his rivalry with his older brother Kay, and his tutelage under Merlyn, the magician who lives life backwards and who on one occasion manages to entangle his knitting with his own beard. The novel, which is infused throughout with an enthusiasm for natural history and country pursuits such as falconry, ends with Wart's transformation into the youthful king of England when he pulls the sword from the stone. Four further volumes followed, to form a five-part collection entitled *The Once and Future King*, running to over 850 pages in modern editions and as epic in its way as its distant ancestors, Malory's *Le Morte d'Arthur* and the French Vulgate Cycle of poems. Other writers who gave their own individual spin on the Arthur stories include Marion Zimmer Bradley, whose 1982 novel *The Mists of Avalon* gave a feminist twist to Arthur's world by championing the women who surround King Arthur; John Cowper Powys, who drew from Welsh history as well as Arthurian legends in *Porius: A Romance of the Dark Ages* (1951), set in Wales immediately before the Saxon invasion; and John Steinbeck, who in 1976 published a respectful rendering of the stories in *The Acts of King Arthur and his Noble Knights*.

Film and musical versions of the stories were also popular. In 1960 T.H. White's novels were adapted into the Lerner and Loewe stage musical *Camelot* and, shortly afterwards, into a cute Walt Disney animated film, under the title *The Sword in the Stone*. Lerner and Loewe's musical, with its focus on the love of Lancelot and Guinevere and the cuckolding of Arthur, was itself made into a disastrously lavish film (under the same title) in 1967. John Boorman's fantasy film *Excalibur* (1981) provides a colourful take on the stories, while Robert Bresson's 1974 film *Lancelot du Lac* wallows in the discomforts and dangers of medieval life, with knights creaking and groaning as they stagger around in heavy armour, and Lancelot and Guinevere conducting their trysts amid drab back rooms or damp haylofts. By this time King Arthur had become such a familiar figure on film that the whole genre was ripe for lampooning, and this came in the form of the comedy spoof *Monty Python and the Holy Grail* (1975), much of which was filmed in the Highlands of Scotland – not exactly part of the country that is replete with Arthurian legends. Some thirty years later the film was reworked by Eric Idle as the stage spoof-musical *Spamalot*, a neat reference to the Python team's obsession with the tinned meat, spam (as in, 'We dine well here in Camelot / We eat ham and jam and spam a lot'). These re-imaginings of the Arthur of medieval romances have played alongside attempts to portray him as a genuine historical figure, in TV series such as *Arthur of the Britons* (1972–73),

Merlin (2008–12), and *The Legend of King Arthur* (1979), and in the feature films *King Arthur* (2004), *The Last Legion* (2007) and *King Arthur: Legend of the Sword* (2017). In the wake of all this popularity Arthur has also been purloined as someone whose code of chivalry and honour can prove inspirational to children. In the United States, hundreds of thousands of boys and girls joined Arthurian youth groups, such as the Knights of King Arthur, in which Arthur's qualities were promoted for children as wholesome exemplars of how lives should be led. As the scholar Norris J. Lacy has observed, 'The popular notion of Arthur appears to be limited, not surprisingly, to a few motifs and names, but there can be no doubt of the extent to which a legend born many centuries ago is profoundly embedded in modern culture at every level'.

King Arthur in the Landscape

Across the road from Cannon Street Station in the City of London, and housed within a smart casing of white marble set into the exterior wall of number 111 Cannon Street, is a block of oolitic limestone of ancient provenance and great mythical and historical significance. The existence of this stone was first recorded in around the year 1100, when it stood outside the now-demolished St Swithun's Church on the same street. In 1598 the historian John Stow described it in his *Survey of London* as 'a great stone called [the] London Stone ... pitched upright ... fixed in the ground verie deep, fastened with bars of iron'. Numerous theories abound as to the origins of the so-called London Stone; was it part of an ancient stone circle? Or a was it a Roman marker stone that pinpointed the exact centre of Londinium? In 1450 Jack Cade, leader of a rebellion against Henry VI, smashed the blade of his sword against the stone and claimed that he was 'lord of the city'. Perhaps this event inspired a legend to grow that that this was the stone from which the boy Arthur pulled a sword that had stuck fast within it, thus anointing himself the rightful King of England. The legend seems to be comparatively recent; even though this stone would have been known to Thomas Malory, it was not the one he was thinking of when he wrote *Morte d'Arthur*, as his stone was marble, not limestone, and Malory seems to have favoured St Paul's as the venue for Arthur's anointing, which is some 500 metres away from Cannon Street. Nonetheless, although stories of King Arthur and his

The London Stone, housed in marble casing in the heart of the City of London, is reputedly the legendary stone from which Arthur drew his sword. (*Andrew Beattie*)

knights have a habit of attaching themselves to similarly monumental stones throughout Britain, the London Stone is the only Arthurian 'site' in London or Southeast England – not surprisingly, perhaps, as this area was firmly occupied by the Saxons in Arthur's time, while the Celtic Britons whom Arthur championed, sheltered in Southwest England, Wales and Scotland.

King Arthur has long been associated with natural and man-made features in the landscape, from mountains and rocky outcrops to prehistoric cairns and medieval castles. For many of these features it is difficult to say when these folkloric associations began, and indeed whether the name 'Arthur' ascribed to them is actually King Arthur, or whether it denotes an entirely different historical personality of the same name. The first text to highlight these associations was the *Mirabilia Britanniae* (*The Wonders of Britain*), a 1,000-word account of the natural marvels of the British Isles that was written around 820 and, in its earliest versions, was appended to the *Historia Brittonum*, the chronicle that was probably written by the Welsh monk, Nennius. Nennius might have written the *Mirabilia* too, and in it, he – or another author – catalogues twenty miracles (*miracula*) and wonders (*mirabilia*) associated with various named locations in the British Isles. Scotland claims one of these miracles or wonders; thirteen are spread across an area that encompasses northeast, southeast and southwest Wales along with the Welsh border regions, the Severn Valley and Bath; four are in Anglesey and two are in Ireland. Two of these features, namely Carn Gafallt and Gamber Head, both in the Welsh Borders, are noted in the *Mirabilia* as having connections to King Arthur – and these comprise the first written records of sites that have acquired a place in Arthurian legend.

Unfortunately both of the Arthurian sites described in the *Mirabilia* are today somewhat elusive. Although Gamber Head, the spring that forms the source of the River Gamber, is easy to find – it's just south of the village of Wormelow in Herefordshire, up against the eastern side of the A466 Hereford to Monmouth road – the tomb of Arthur's son Amr, which the *Mirabilia* claims is near by, has vanished from the map. 'Amr [was] the son of the warrior Arthur, who killed him in that place and buried him,' the *Mirabilia* explains – in a tomb that was invested with magical properties. 'Men come to measure the grave and find it sometimes six feet in length, sometimes nine, sometimes twelve, sometimes fifteen. At whatever length you might measure it at one time, a second time you will not find it to have the same length'. The tomb or burial mound in question was probably Wormelow Tump, which was flattened in 1896 to create what is now the A466. The tump is recalled in the name of the Tump Inn in Wormelow village, whose sign depicts King Arthur brandishing a sword, with something looking like a burial mound in the background.

Carn Gafallt, the second site in the *Mirabilia* with an Arthurian connection, is a natural rather than a man-made feature. It's a gorse-covered mountain situated in wild countryside between Rhayader and Builth Wells in east-central Wales. According to the *Mirabilia*, the site consists of a pile of stones, with – placed on top – a hard rock in which the pawprint of a dog is mysteriously imprinted. This is the footprint of Cafall, Arthur's dog, and it was apparently made when Arthur was with Cafall in these forests, hunting the boar Trwyd. Unfortunately, although walkers can reach the summit cairns of Carn Gafallt, Cafall's pawprint is somewhat elusive. In the 1840s Lady Charlotte Guest, translator and publisher of the ancient Welsh text known as the *Mabinogion*, apparently persuaded a gentleman of her acquaintance (whose name she never revealed) to climb the mountain and look for it. Lady Charlotte's correspondent duly confirmed that,

The Tump Inn at Wormelow, whose name recalls the burial mound of Arthur's son Amr. (*Source, Andy Dolman, Wikimedia Commons*)

on one of [the summit] cairns may still be seen a stone, so nearly corresponding with the description in Nennius, as to furnish strong presumption that it is the identical object referred to. It is near two feet in length, and not quite a foot wide, and such as a man might, without any great exertion, carry away in his hands. On the one side is an oval indentation, rounded at the bottom, nearly four inches long by three wide, about two inches deep, and altogether presenting such an appearance as might, without any great strain of imagination, be thought to resemble the print of a dog's foot.

However, recent expeditions by those trying to find what Lady Charlotte's gentleman friend apparently discovered, have proved fruitless – which makes one wonder whether this anonymous nineteenth-century gentleman ever saw this legendary pawprint in the first place.

Since the time of the writing of the *Mirabilia*, hundreds more sites have been invested with Arthurian legend. By the Middle Ages these

Arthurian sites formed a prominent part of Arthuriana in their own right, complementing how Arthur was portrayed in both the literary and folkloric imagination of the day. Often a site's Arthurian connection was grafted on to an already existing folkloric tale – for instance the idea that a king is asleep inside a cave or mountain, ready to rise again, is a folk tale seen in many ancient societies that, in some instances, became associated with King Arthur. Early tales attached to these places often see Arthur as a giant who was able to construct large stones into natural features or otherwise inexplicable prehistoric monuments; later stories relate to parts of the Arthurian tradition that were introduced in the Middle Ages, such as the Round Table or the quest for the Holy Grail. The connection with Arthur is never anything more than tenuous; indeed this is acknowledged at the sites themselves – 'legend tells', say the once-colourful information boards, fading in the wind and the rain, or, 'according to local tradition', or 'some say'. The stories associated with these places are variously romantic, magical, violent, or tragic; many are improbable, and none can be proved. Yet such tales provide local colour and, having been built up by a succession of storytellers each propagating their own agenda, are reflective of the time and society in which they were first told. It is the purpose of the remainder of this book to provide a description of these sites, spread as they are across the British Isles, France and Italy, with Cornwall and the West Country counties of Somerset, Dorset and Wiltshire providing the primary focus. And even if the tales attached to these locations are fanciful and inaccurate they are no less entertaining and inventive for that, as the accounts of the sites in this book will reveal.

Part Two

THE PLACES ASSOCIATED WITH KING ARTHUR

Out of all the great Arthurian sites of Britain, two stand out. They are Tintagel, a promontory – well, virtually an island – on the remote, storm-lashed coast of north Cornwall, where according to the medieval historian Geoffrey of Monmouth, King Arthur was conceived, in dark and magical circumstances; and Glastonbury, in Somerset, where, in the late twelfth century, monks at the local abbey claimed to have made an astonishing discovery – that of the final resting place of Arthur and his queen, Guinevere. Tintagel and Glastonbury set the tone for their respective counties, for both Cornwall and Somerset are crammed with sites that claim some sort of connection with the mythical Dark Age ruler; together they form the two epicentres of geographical Arthuriana. Today these two places milk their Arthurian connections for all they are worth; in fact Tintagel risks condemning itself to a bland existence as something akin to an Arthurian theme park. Yet for the purposes of this book Tintagel and Glastonbury provide a geographical focus for a narrative of Arthur's life; for one of these places marks where it began, the other where it ended. Between his birth at Tintagel and burial at Glastonbury, Arthur – according to the most significant chroniclers – held court at Camelot and fought a series of great battles, the last and most important being at Camlann. The location of Camelot has vexed Arthur 'historians' for centuries, with various locations in South Wales, Cornwall and Somerset, as well as Winchester and sites in the North of England, all making some historical claim to be the 'genuine' place where Arthur gathered together his faithful knights around his celebrated Round Table. As for Camlann, Slaughterbridge near the town of Camelford in Cornwall seems to make the strongest claim as being the site of that fateful battle, though there are plenty of other contenders. When these places are plotted across a map of the southwest of England, a geographical narrative of Arthur's life emerges; from his conception and birth, to the glory of his rule, to his defeat in battle, and finally to his death and burial. A description of all these locations forms the focus of this central part of the book, presented in the logical narrative arc of Arthur's life; and this means that we need to open with an account of what is probably the most famous Arthurian site of all.

Chapter One

The Conception and Birth of King Arthur

Tintagel, Damelioc and Stonehenge

'Most of us,' wrote the avid Arthurian and Cornwall resident L.J. Dickinson in his self-published 1949 guide to Tintagel, *The Story of King Arthur in Cornwall*,

> find when we have lived in Cornwall some time, we have gradually developed a belief in many things at which formerly we should have scoffed, [and] end up by believing, sometimes even by knowing, that many things are true which cannot be explained by ordinary means, and which were formerly not dreamt of in our philosophy.

Dickinson's booklet – a classic production of post-war austerity, with no photographs and its text set tightly on the page to reduce the amount of paper used – goes on to claim that the 'tales of King Arthur, of Merlin, of the Round Table, and of the Holy Grail, take hold of us; and though we know that many of the stories are fabulous, and others are much garbled, nothing shakes our conviction that King Arthur was born at Tintagel'. Although the booklet claims to be 'published for the use of tourists visiting Tintagel' it is not really a guide to the castle in the usual sense; rather, it is a paean to Cornwall and the Arthurian legends associated with the county, particularly Tintagel, the setting that Geoffrey of Monmouth chose for the story of Arthur's mysterious and magical conception. In the second part of the booklet, Dickinson tries to persuade the reader of the historical veracity of Arthur, adhering to the pervasive current of thought of the time. 'It is true that the [Welsh] triads say little,' Dickinson admits, but there is sufficient evidence in them that Arthur really lived. [Yet] surely the great stories of Tintagel about Arthur and his knights, and about Merlin and the Round Table, could not have persisted for these fourteen hundred years unless they had some foundation … even local nomenclature testifies to the existence of Arthur – for why otherwise should places be named after him!

(Dickinson cites as 'evidence' for this the rock formation known as Arthur's Hall on Bodmin Moor and the coastal promontory known as Arthur's headland.) Dickinson concludes that,

We can scarcely doubt that there did live a very great man who was called Arthur, who was a defender of Christianity and civilisation at a time when both were nearly overwhelmed in Britain by Teutonic barbarism … always did he contend against this advancing hosts of Teutonic pagans, who were devastating and appropriating the land, as the Germans in our day swept over Belgium and parts of France. We read of cities burnt and churches destroyed, exactly as their descendants laid waste the beautiful towns of France and Belgium.

This purloining of the legend of Arthur to suit the agenda of a particular time – Dickinson identifies Arthur as a British hero who saw off the encroaching Saxon (for which read, German) hordes from across the North Sea – was nothing new. In the 1940s Arthur was often depicted as the nationalist hero who had fought the Germanic invaders; back in the late Middle Ages writers found that this familiar figure from folklore could easily embody the necessary characteristics of the age of chivalry, through subtle (or not-so-subtle) alterations in his character traits and the narrative into which he fits. When Geoffrey of Monmouth was compiling his pseudo-historical *History of the Kings of England* in the 1130s, during the golden age of knights in shining armour and all the other accoutrements of the Age of Chivalry, Arthur also fulfilled a political agenda – in fact two separate agendas, which were set in direct opposition to each other. Geoffrey created his Arthur myth just six decades after the wholesale revolution of the Norman invasion (he wrote his work during the reign of William the Conqueror's younger son, Henry I). It's during times of political and social trauma such as an invasion that the past becomes a place of refuge. Arthur garnered popularity among the Anglo-Saxons of a defeated England as a hero who had resisted foreign invaders (despite the fact that it was them he was fighting), and this must still have been an abiding cultural tenet when Geoffrey concocted his *History*. Yet conversely, Arthur was also a hero to the Normans, who were still busily constructing a post-Conquest England when Geoffrey was at work; they saw in King Arthur a beguiling hero who had the gall to take on the Anglo-Saxons, who were their enemy as well as his – and they enthusiastically embraced him. In this way both the conquerors and the vanquished of twelfth-century England had a hero from the distant and mystical past that they could avidly celebrate and venerate. So Geoffrey's tale had a ready-made audience, even before he started writing it.

Why Tintagel?

In summary, Geoffrey of Monmouth's tale of Arthur's conception tells of how, through the magic of Merlin, a warrior named Uther Pendragon impregnates Arthur's mother Igerna after disguising himself as Gorlois, her husband, through a spell woven by the magician Merlin. Why Geoffrey of Monmouth specifically chose Tintagel as the place where this drama was played out is unclear. In the twelfth century this must have been one of the wildest and most remote spots in England; a blustery promontory on Cornwall's rugged north coast, pounded by the crashing waves of the Atlantic, a part of the mainland but only just. (Somewhat romantically, the site of Tintagel is often referred to as an 'island', but in reality, in the Middle Ages, the site could be accessed by a narrow isthmus of land that tethered it to the cliffs that line this part of the coast; this isthmus is now long-collapsed, a victim of waves and storms and landslips, and today a precipitous ravine, traversed by a controversial new pedestrian suspension bridge, separates the promontory of Tintagel from the mainland.) Did Geoffrey himself ever come here? There is certainly no evidence that he did. But he might well have been told about the site by a traveller who traversed pock-marked medieval tracks or who braved the heaving seas of the Atlantic to reach this spot by boat, perhaps from a port such as Minehead or Bristol. Alternatively, Geoffrey might have read about the place from various historical sources; many have suggested that Tintagel might be the place then known as Rosnant, meaning the 'headland by the valley', which appears in a number of early Irish historical texts (and is an apt description that can be applied very obviously to Tintagel, where access to the promontory on which the castle sits is through a deep cleft with precipitous sides). He might, too, have known that Tintagel was an important political centre of the Dark Ages, and for this reason selected it to play an important part in his story. But even more likely is that he knew Tintagel played an important role in another Cornwall-set story of mysticism and magic – that of Tristan and Iseult.

The origins of the story of Tristan are as hard to pin down as those of Arthur. In the late twelfth century – a few decades after Geoffrey's *History* – a Norman poet known only as Béroul set parts of his tale of Tristan and Iseult in Tintagel. One part of the drama of Tristan that was played out in the castle was the hero's conception. Like any writer in any age, Béroul was working within a set of expected and accepted conventions, one of which was a tradition of 'birth of a hero' stories that stretched back into antiquity. Similar tales can be found in Irish and even Indian literature and tradition. It is possible that Béroul simply translated the substance of these stories from the wilds of Ireland or the deserts of Persia to the rocky coast of Cornwall. According to Béroul's narrative, Tintagel served as the ruling seat of King Mark of Cornwall during Tristan's time; Tristan was Mark's nephew and Iseult (or Isolde), with whom Tristan fell in love, was Mark's queen. Béroul's *Tristan* post-dates Geoffrey's work by a few decades, so it cannot have influenced Geoffrey in his decision to set parts of the Arthur story there. Yet what if Béroul was working from a source that is now lost, that placed the narrative of Tristan's conception in Tintagel, and which was also known to Geoffrey? If this was the case then we have an answer as to why Geoffrey was so drawn to the site; the place where Tristan was conceived easily served Geoffrey's narrative as the place where Arthur was conceived. But whatever Tintagel meant to Geoffrey of Monmouth – whether he knew it to be a historical seat of Dark Age power, or the fabled residence of a half-mythical Cornish king and his lovestruck nephew, or the place where that lovestruck nephew was conceived – this was where he chose to set his mystical tale of the conception of King Arthur.

Tintagel in the Dark Ages

History runs deep along the north coast of Cornwall. From earliest times the succession of high rocky ridges that project like gnarled and

The promontory on which the settlement of Tintagel was founded, with the western entrance to Merlin's Cave bottom right. (*Andrew Beattie*)

crooked fingers into the churning sea proved ideal defensive positions; flanked on three sides by the Atlantic, their fourth, and landward, side could easily be defended through the digging of a deep ditch. Any raiders would be faced with the impossible choice of attacking across this ditch, or approaching the settlement from the sea – which meant confronting storm-lashed cliffs and heavy seas. During the Iron Age (roughly 700 BC to AD 50) settlements on sites like these were common along the coastlines of Wales and Cornwall, and it is possible that Tintagel was occupied at this time by one such settlement – though the site has yielded nothing by way of evidence. On the 'mainland' to which the promontory of Tintagel is tethered an earthwork is visible known simply as the 'great ditch'. This is a deep grassy trough in the landscape that might have Iron Age origins, separating as it does the narrow promontory of Tintagel from the mainland (today it runs between the upper ticket booth and the buildings housing the main shop and visitor centre). In the end it is unclear what sort of settlement – if any – occupied the Tintagel promontory at the end of the Iron Age, when the Romans invaded Britain and incorporated Cornwall into the economic, political and social structures of their Empire. The conquerors were particularly interested in Cornwall as it gave them control over tin mining, which was what had attracted them to Britain in the first place (tin being a vital component in bronze, from which weapons were fashioned). But evidence for Roman occupation of the Tintagel site is nearly as scant as that from the Iron Age. It consists largely of inscribed stones such as the one that has ended up in Tintagel Parish Church that bears the inscription 'IMP C G VAL LIC LICIN', which is the name of Caius Flavius Valerius Licinianus Licinius, who was executed by the Emperor Constantine in AD 324 as a rival claimant to his throne; the stone was either a milestone or was set up as a sign of Roman authority in the camp established on the nearby cliffs.

All of which brings us to the Dark Ages, the great expanse of history that descended on Britain when the Romans departed in the early fifth century, in which the legend of Arthur took root. It is clear from archaeological evidence – including both artefacts and buildings – that around a century after the departure of the Romans, Tintagel had become a major centre of settlement, trade and power. For the casual visitor to Tintagel the evidence for this is clearest in the rectangular footprints of buildings – most of them consisting of knee-high walls that are smothered with a generous dollop of turf – that scatter the site, clinging to natural ledges and often looking as if they are about to slide down the vertical cliffs and be lost to the waves (a fate that, over time, has actually befallen many of the Tintagel ruins). The most prominent of these rectangular ruins lie just beyond Richard of Cornwall's medieval castle, which will be discussed shortly; from a distance it is possible to see similar crumbling rectangles of stone, the footprints of buildings that are rendered inaccessible by their locations at the edge of steep precipices. As well as clinging to the sloping edges of the promontory, the Dark Age ruins also cover its flatter top; many of these remains were exposed by a fire in 1983 that burned much of the surface turf away to reveal the stone footprints of buildings just below the surface. It is unknown what these buildings were used for, but it is clear that at the time when King Arthur is widely supposed to have flourished – in the years either side of AD 500 – Tintagel had a substantial population. The structures whose remains can be seen today are of stone, but they might have replaced earlier timber buildings, shown by evidence of post-holes set into the bedrock.

In the summer of 2017, archaeologists investigating the southern cliffs of the promontory – a wild location set apart from most of the Tintagel ruins – made a discovery that confirmed what many believed already: that during the Dark Ages Tintagel was not only a major settlement, it was a prominent political centre too. The buildings unearthed during this dig are very different to those that scatter the rest of the island, with well-built, substantial walls made of slate that were arranged around a large, open courtyard. It is assumed these buildings were a palace of some kind; only those of high status could afford to house themselves in such comparatively extravagant surroundings. And on the last day of the dig, just as archaeologists were preparing to wrap their excavations in protective covering for the winter, a remarkable find was made here, taking the form of a large, flattened piece of stone that had been utilised as a windowsill. Remarkably, writing was scratched into the stone – not formal inscriptions but random, untidy jottings that, though badly weathered, seem to spell out the Roman name Tito and another name, Budic, which was a common name in Breton and Cornish. Could the writer of the words have been an inscriber of monuments, and had merely used this slab for a bit of idle practice? Either way, the find confirmed (in stone) that Dark Age Tintagel was occupied by a literate, Christian elite who led a largely extravagant and peaceful lifestyle.

The wealth of that elite – which underpinned their political power, as expressed in the newly uncovered buildings on the promontory's south side – came from trade. Dark Age Britain was not the inward-looking place that we sometimes imagine, and in those days Tintagel was not the remote and isolated fastness that a casual glance at its location might otherwise suggest. Archaeological finds across the promontory include huge quantities of pottery fragments that are the remains of luxury goods imported from the Mediterranean; in fact Tintagel has by far the largest collection of imported pottery of any known site in Britain, and it is clear that the settlement formed a key part of a trading network that reached as far as the Eastern Mediterranean. Key artefacts unearthed include shards from amphorae, the large, double-handed vessels that were used to carry olive oil or wine, and which were manufactured in the eastern Mediterranean; Phocaean Red Slip pottery, originating from Turkey; and glass vessels manufactured around Bordeaux. Many of these finds can now be seen in the Royal Cornwall Museum in Truro, the county's premier museum. Ranged in an elegant nineteenth-century hall in the city centre, the exhibits in this rambling but absorbing museum cover everything from a world-class collection of multi-hued minerals to a fully-wrapped Egyptian mummy and a gallery of paintings of Cornish landscapes. The finds from Tintagel are limited to a single case that contains curving fragments of pastel-pink, sandy-red and dusty-cream earthenware shards that are from amphora manufactured on the Greek islands of Rhodes, Chios and Kos, and in North Africa and Southwestern Turkey. (One piece of red-slip tableware from Phocaea, an ancient Greek city near present-day Izmir on the west coast of Turkey, has been reassembled to show its original form; a wide, shallow bowl that might perhaps have been a large communal bowl intended to contain fruit or soup.) It is thought that the ships that brought these items to Tintagel, anchoring in the rocky cove below the castle that, in fine weather, makes for an ideal natural harbour, and then returned to Europe and the Middle East laden with tin and Celtic slaves.

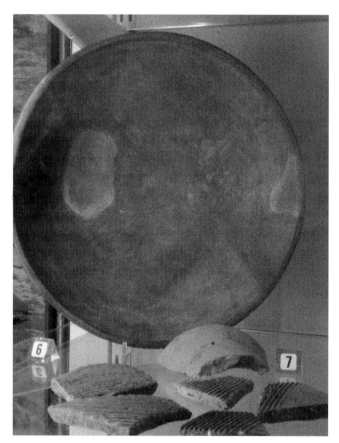

Reassembled tableware from Phocaea, an ancient Greek city, found in Tintagel and now on display in the Royal Cornwall Museum in Truro. (*Andrew Beattie*)

For those who exercised power from here, Tintagel was highly defendable as well as being an ideal site for trade; and so it became a crucial power base – perhaps even the most important power base – of the rulers of the Celtic kingdom of Dumnonia, which incorporated modern-day Cornwall, Devon and parts of Somerset. In true Dark Age tradition very little is known of this ancient kingdom. Only two of Dumnonia's kings are known by name; Constantine and Gerent. The chronicler Gildas wrote of the former that he was a murderer and an enemy of Christian life – damning him as a 'tyrant whelp [youth] of the filthy lioness of Dumnonia'. The kingdom survived until around 708, when the lands east of the Tamar were annexed by the Anglo-Saxon King of Wessex, who left Gerent to rule over what is now Cornwall (which held out against the encroaching Saxons until 838). By that time the first legends of a long-ago ruler of the Britons who flourished in these parts were beginning to emerge.

Tintagel remains the subject of on-going archaeological investigations, but none reach the extent of those supervised in the 1930s by the leading archaeologist Ralegh Radford, who had a life-long association with the site; he began excavations here in 1933 and published his first guide two years later, and in the years before the Second World War he would enthusiastically address visitors about his latest finds. During the war he abandoned Cornwall for the balmier climes of Algiers, where he served as a chief intelligence officer, but afterwards he returned to archaeology and he was still active in Cornwall in 1990, when at the age of 90 he surveyed Tintagel by helicopter (he died eight years later at the age of 98). Grand old man of Tintagel archaeology he may have been, but since Radford's death a number of his key theories about the site have been gently put aside. One was that he had uncovered here the remains of an early Christian monastery; this notion was taught to several generations of archaeology students but has since been discounted, partly by the major fire in 1983, which uncovered much that had been previously hidden below turf, and partly through analysis of finds made during large-scale excavations under the direction of Professor Christopher Morris of Glasgow University, which begun in 1990. Another of Radford's assertions was that parts of the medieval castle that now stand on the promontory were built in the 1140s by Reginald, Earl of Cornwall, the illegitimate son of Henry I (and grandson of William the Conqueror) – placing the construction of the castle a century earlier than is now accepted. If Reginald, Earl of Cornwall, had indeed built part of the castle then its construction would have been contemporaneous with Geoffrey of Monmouth's seminal *Historia*. But Radford's theories have been discounted by the fact that no twelfth-century pottery has been found at Tintagel – and by the lack of any written references to the site until the year 1200.

King Arthur's conception at Tintagel

It is the ruins of the medieval castle that supply Tintagel's romantic mystique. The much earlier remains of the Dark Age buildings rarely rise above knee-height, but the stone skeleton of the castle forms a pleasing jumble of substantial walls, toothy crenellations and intact archways on the promontory, while on the mainland even more robust walls enclose large, rectangular courtyards that spread over flat ledges at the top of precipitous cliffs. But it is the clutch of ruins on the promontory that fire the imagination; clinging to a vertiginous cliff and slowly crumbling into the crashing waves below, the ancient stonework appears to sprout from the rock from which the promontory is formed, so organically does the castle appear to be fused with it. The ruins here are not substantial, and consist mainly of a small medieval Great Hall and various associated buildings (latrines, kitchens, and so on), but all of it is framed so spectacularly above the rocky cove, with views beyond to the inlets and rocky headlands along the coastline, that it is difficult not to be captivated by the place. It is these ruins, these cliffs, this view of the coast, that lie at the heart of Arthurian romance in Cornwall. The writer Arthur Mee (1875–1943), whose fiercely patriotic works for children such as *The King's England* and *The Children's Encyclopaedia* are now deeply unfashionable in an age that is proudly cynical about that sort of thing, summed up the romantic appeal of Tintagel when he wrote that, 'In the evening, when the sun is sinking into the Atlantic from something like a flaming battlefield, we can think it is true about Arthur and his knights. A deep sense of something mysterious comes upon us.' And yet the castle is a fake; a phoney, built centuries after the supposed time of King Arthur by one of the wealthiest men in England who was drawn to this site on account of nothing more than a flight of fancy wrought by a medieval spinner of elaborate tales that masqueraded as history.

The account by Geoffrey of Monmouth – that medieval spinner of tales – concerning the miraculous conception of King Arthur opens with Arthur's supposed grandfather, Constantine, declaring himself Roman Emperor.

This was not Constantine the Great, whose mother was St Helena, but a lesser-known and much later emperor of the same name, Constantine III, who declared himself Western Roman Emperor in 407 at a time of schism and turmoil in the dying Empire (though in his *History* Geoffrey seems to have conflated Constantine III with the Constantine who ruled the kingdom of Dumnonia in around 520). In declaring himself Emperor, Constantine defies the Emperor Honorus, who was ruling the eastern empire from Rome. Constantine's enthronement is celebrated by British warlords in Silchester, which was in those days an important Roman settlement close to the banks of the River Kennet near Reading; they perform his coronation with elaborate ceremony, and, at the same time, celebrate his marriage to a lady that Geoffrey does not name but claims is 'descended from a noble Roman family'. Constantine then heads across the English Channel to confront the forces of Honorus in France, as the Roman Empire crumbles around both rival Emperors.

The union between Constantine and his un-named wife eventually produces three sons, who are named Constans, Aurelius Ambrosius, and Uther Pendragon. On the death of Constantine, Vortigern, one of the great tribal leaders of Britain, asks Constans to assume the throne – but treacherously attempts to capture it himself, as he believes Constans is too feeble a personality to grip firmly the reins of power. Constans 'bore the title of king,' Geoffrey explains, but 'was no more than the shadow of one; for he was of a soft temper, a bad judge in matters of right, and not in the least feared, either by his own people, or by the neighbouring states'. Vortigern has Constans assassinated and his severed head brought to him as proof that he is dead; fearing that they are next, Aurelius and Uther flee to Brittany, but later return to take revenge on Vortigern for the death of their brother Constans. They land at Totnes in Devon, and Aurelius's revenge is indeed sweet; he causes Vortigern to be burned alive, and succeeds him as king, but he in turn is poisoned by a treacherous Saxon, leaving his brother Uther to confront the deadly enemy alone. Uther harries bands of Saxons across the north of England but is vigorously beaten back, and decides to hold court with other British leaders at a hill named Damen, which according to Geoffrey was 'high, and had a hazel-wood upon the top of it, and about the middle broken and cavernous rocks, which were a harbour to wild beasts.' One leader who stands out at this gathering is Gorlois, who advises a surprise attack on the Saxons. Uther acts on his advice and the attack proves successful. He goes on to pacify the Scots and eventually meets again with the other leaders, this time in London, where once again he encounters Gorlois.

Uther's second meeting with Gorlois is the narrative spark that begins the sequence of events leading to Arthur's conception. This time, when Uther meets Gorlois, the warlord has his wife Igerna with him – and Uther takes an immediate fancy to her. (In Thomas Malory's version of the same story, which follows Geoffrey's pretty closely, Igerna is known as Igraine.) 'No sooner had [Uther] cast his eyes upon her among the rest of the ladies, than he fell passionately in love with her, and little regarding the rest, made her the subject of all his thoughts,' Geoffrey narrates. 'She was the only lady that he continually served with fresh dishes, and to whom he sent golden cups by his confidants; on her he bestowed all his smiles, and to her he addressed all his discourse.' Gorlois, angry at the attention that Uther is piling on his wife, retires from the court and heads for his dukedom in Cornwall; incensed by the snub of his departure, Uther commands him to return – but Gorlois refuses. So Uther prepares to square up to him in battle. 'Accordingly, without delay, while their anger was hot against each other, the king [Uther] got together a great army, and marched into Cornwall, the cities and towns whereof he set on fire,' Geoffrey narrates. Gorlois finds himself on the run.

> [He] durst not engage with Uther, on account of the inferiority of his numbers; and thought it a wiser course to fortify his towns, till he could get succour from Ireland. And as he was under more concern for his wife than himself, he put her into the town of Tintagel, upon the sea-shore, which he looked upon as a place of great safety.

With Igerna safe (and safely out of the way) in Tintagel, Gorlois entrenches himself at another of his fortresses, Damelioc (known in Malory's version as Castle Terrible); this tactic prevented him and Igerna 'being both at once involved in the same danger, if any should happen'.

Geoffrey's reference to the 'town of Tintagel' would presumably have meant the settlement that in those days covered the promontory; there was no castle at Tintagel at the time – castles as we know them did not appear in England until the eleventh century – but as we know, there was a reasonably substantial settlement spread out between the cliffs on the promontory, complete with public buildings and possibly a palace. This, presumably, was where Igerna took refuge. The village now known as Tintagel, on the 'mainland', would at that time have consisted of a few shacks or farms – if, indeed, the site was settled at all in the Dark Ages. As for Uther, even as he laid siege to Gorlois's army at Damelioc, his passion for Igerna continued to torment him. Geoffrey's account indicates that he 'said to one of his confidants, named Ulfin de Ricaradoch, 'My passion for Igerna is such, that I can neither have ease of mind, nor health of body, till I obtain her; and if you cannot assist me with your advice how to accomplish my desire, the inward torments I endure will kill me.' Ulfin replied thus:

> Who can advise you in this matter … when no force will enable us to have access to her in the town of Tintagel? For it is situated upon the sea, and on every side surrounded by it; and there is but one entrance into it, and that through a straight rock, which three men shall be able to defend against the whole power of the kingdom. Notwithstanding, if the prophet Merlin would in earnest set about this attempt, I am of opinion, you might with his advice obtain your wishes.

Merlin, who had travelled to Cornwall with Uther's army, 'finding the great anguish of the king, was moved by such excessive love' – and suggested a plan that was, of course, infused with magic. 'To accomplish your desire,' Merlin told Uther,

> you must make use of such arts as have not been heard of in your time. I know how, by the force of my medicines, to give you the exact likeness of Gorlois, so that in all respects you shall seem to be no other than himself. If you will therefore obey my prescriptions, I will metamorphose you into the true semblance of Gorlois, and Ulfin into Jordan of Tintagel, his familiar friend; and I myself, being transformed into another shape, will make the third in the adventure; and in this disguise you may go safely to the town where Igerna is, and have admittance to her.

So Uther avails himself of Merlin's potions and in their disguises the three of them head for Tintagel. Geoffrey relates that,

> they arrived in the evening twilight, and forthwith signified to the porter, that the consul was come; upon which the gates were opened, and the men let in. For what room could there

be for suspicion, when Gorlois himself seemed to be there present? The king therefore stayed that night with Igerna, and had the full enjoyment of her, for she was deceived with the false disguise which he had put on, and the artful and amorous discourses wherewith he entertained her ... The same night therefore she conceived of the most renowned Arthur, whose heroic and wonderful actions have justly rendered his name famous to posterity.

And thus Arthur is conceived through Igerna's union with Uther, who through Merlin's magical devices appears to her as her husband Gorlois. (This crucial part of the story may have been inspired by an ancient Greek myth, in which Alexander the Great is conceived when a King of Egypt named Nectanebus disguises himself as another man and impregnates Philip of Macedon's wife while Philip is away fighting; a similar story from Ireland also tells of the conception of a hero named Mongán, who was fathered by the Irish sea-god Manannán who slept with the wife of the warrior Fiachnae mac Báetáin while Fiachnae was away fighting in battle.)

Uther's army, meanwhile, attack Damelioc without him. They are successful and the real Gorlois is killed. Messengers are at once dispatched to Igerna with the bad news. When they reach Tintagel they are surprised to see Gorlois alive and well and speaking with Igerna! Of course the person they see is not Gorlois but Uther, still disguised as him; Igerna realises that she has been tricked, though she does not know exactly how. (Later embellishments of Geoffrey's tale indicate that Merlin restores Uther back to his original appearance by washing him in a stream of running water; legend has it that the brook in question was the one that winds down the Trebarwith Valley just a couple of miles south of Tintagel.) However, Geoffrey does relate that when Uther comes to Igerna again, this time as himself and with no disguise, she consents to marry him. 'After this,' Geoffrey maintains, 'they continued to live together [in Tintagel] with much affection for each other, and had a son and daughter, whose names were Arthur and Anne.'

The accounts of Geoffrey and Malory diverge here, with Malory offering a more colourful version of what happened next. According to Malory, Merlin tells Uther that he knows 'a lord of yours in this land ... and he shall have the nourishing of your child, and his name is Sir Ector' – and suggests that Arthur is brought up by him. So,

when the lady was delivered, the king commanded two
knights and two ladies to take the child, bound in a cloth
of gold ... So the child was delivered unto Merlin, and so
he bare it forth unto Sir Ector, and made an holy man to
christen him, and named him Arthur.

Thus Sir Ector takes Arthur and brings him up as his own son. Arthur's
upbringing accounted for, both authors' narratives now once again
converge. Soon after Arthur's birth, Uther falls ill and is forced to take
command of the next battle against the Saxons lying on a specially-made
litter (Malory indicates that this battle is fought at St Albans). Uther's
army is victorious but Uther, like his brother Aurelius before him, is
murdered by his Saxon foes, who poison the well from which he is often
known to drink. According to Malory Uther dies and is buried in London,
but this time it is Geoffrey of Monmouth who spins a more colourful
tale than Malory, for he has Uther buried beside Aurelius at a place he
enigmatically refers to as the 'Giant's Dance'.

Stonehenge and Damelioc

The 'Giant's Dance' where, according to Geoffrey of Monmouth, Uther
and Aurelius were buried is known to us as Stonehenge. Geoffrey of
Monmouth maintained that the monument, thought by archaeologists to
have been constructed from around 2400 BC onwards, was in fact built
by Uther's brother Aurelius in honour of his comrades who had fallen in
battle against the Saxons. But the suggestion that this memorial should
take the form of Stonehenge is made by Merlin, who instructs Aurelius to,

send for the Giant's Dance, which is in Killaraus, a mountain
in Ireland. For there is a structure of stones there, which
none of this age could raise, without a profound knowledge
of the mechanical arts. They are stones of a vast magnitude
and wonderful quality; and if they can be placed here, as they
are there, round this spot of ground, they will stand for ever.

Merlin claims that the stones have a 'medicinal virtue', for 'the giants
of old brought them from the farthest coast of Africa, and placed them

A number of Arthurian legends are attached to Stonehenge. (*Source, Frédéric Vincent, Wikimedia Commons*)

in Ireland, while they inhabited that country. Their design in this was to make baths in them, when they should be taken with any illness.' The stones are duly brought from Ireland to Salisbury Plain by 15,000 men – with a little help from Merlin, whose magical 'contrivances' allow them to be transported to ships waiting to take them across the sea to Britain. (When Wace translated and embellished Geoffrey's narrative he added a giant to the story, who helps Merlin erect the stones.) And thus the stones, arranged in circles, form a suitable resting place for Uther and Aurelius, the father and uncle of King Arthur (though according to local tradition, Aurelius is actually buried at Coneybury Hill close by).

Today the Henge, with its pagan associations, is very much associated with King Arthur. Indeed it is occasionally the haunt of a former British soldier turned professional druid who has legally changed his name to King Arthur Uther Pendragon, and regularly holds gatherings among the stones with his white-robed followers, in a celebration of the contemporary New Age-Celtic-Pagan mystical miasma in which the legend of King Arthur now swirls. The associations are not new. In 1926 an amateur archaeologist named Colonel William Hawley unearthed a skeleton from the perimeter of the Henge, and ascertained that the cause of death had been decapitation from a sword blow to the back of the neck; some thirty-five years later a Welsh dentist named Wystan Peach had the body radiocarbon dated and, when it was discovered to date from around AD 650, wrote a pamphlet claiming that this was the body of King Arthur, even though no ancient sources have ever claimed this as his burial place.

As for Damelioc – the fort in which Gorlois holed himself up while pursued by Uther – a number of sites in Cornwall have been suggested as its location. The most arresting is Castle-an-Dinas, a massive Iron Age fort close to the village of St Columb Major, a few miles inland from Newquay. Though no structures stand here today (the site's few visitors must find the title 'castle' very misleading), the circular earthworks (consisting of ditches and banks) are substantial, and this is one of the largest and most intact Iron Age forts in southwest England. Just as striking are the views from the barren, windswept 214 metre high summit, which seem to stretch right across Cornwall in a magnificent 360 degree panorama. In the Dark Ages the view would have been over the trade routes that threaded across these rolling hills; these days it's the alternative energy production (solar farms and wind turbines) that most draw the eye, along with the steady succession of planes making their final approach to Newquay airport, just over the horizon. Excavations in the 1960s revealed that Castle-an-Dinas

Defensive banks and ditches at Castle-an-Dinas, an Iron Age fort near Newquay, and possibly the site of Gorlois's fortress of Damelioc. (*Andrew Beattie*)

was occupied between 400 BC and AD 150, with shards of pottery and postholes for timber houses being the major finds. Unfortunately there was no evidence of prolonged occupation during the supposed time of King Arthur (when, legend has it, this was his hunting lodge) – and indeed the association of this fort with the site of Damelioc seems only to have begun in the Middle Ages. Before that time it was the village of St Dennis, just a mile or so to the south, that claimed to be the site of Gorlois's fortress. Here there is vastly less to see than at Castle-an-Dinas; in fact all that is there is a churchyard that occupies the site of a former defensive settlement (the name of this village, and the church, are derived from the Cornish 'dinas', meaning 'fort', and not from the French St Denis, despite the church being dedicated to this saint). However, the Domesday Survey of 1086 records that a manor in the Parish of St Dennis was called Dimelihoc, which may lend veracity to St Dennis's claims to have been the true Damelioc. A third and final contender for Damelioc is an Iron Age site known as the Tregeare Rounds, situated close to Pendogget, a linear village that straddles the main road that threads through north Cornwall. The site is pretty low-key, with banks and ditches and not much else; in fact some scholars think that the Rounds were never a fort and the site was used instead as a cattle enclosure.

Richard of Cornwall and Tintagel's Medieval Castle

Seal of Richard, Earl of Cornwall, the builder of the castle at Tintagel. (*Source, Wikimedia Commons*)

In the decades following the widespread distribution of Geoffrey of Monmouth's *Historia*, the myth of King Arthur and Tintagel seeped into the medieval consciousness – while, at the same time, the literary Arthur himself embarked on a transformation at the hands of writers, from battle-scarred Dark Age warrior into a chivalrous ruler surrounded by loyal knights. One man who was seduced by the enigma of Arthur was Richard, Earl of Cornwall (1209–72), the second son of King John. Around a century after

Geoffrey of Monmouth's *Historia* first appeared, Richard built a fabulous castle at Tintagel – on the basis, it would seem, of nothing but its fanciful and legendary connection with Britain's legendary Dark Age ruler. Richard festooned his fantasy fortress with battlements, yet the castle had no strategic or defensive value whatsoever. Instead it was an ostentatious statement in stone of Richard's power and wealth – and one that also gave him an opportunity to wrap himself in Arthurian fantasy.

At the time of the castle's construction, Richard was one of the wealthiest and most powerful men in England. He was apparently saturated in Arthurian myth – as indeed was his immediate family. The famous Round Table that still hangs in the Great Hall of Winchester Castle was commissioned either by his brother, King Henry III, or his nephew, Edward I, and Edward I actively honoured the spirit of Arthur when he defeated the Welsh prince Llewellyn, claiming that he had 'recovered Arthur's crown'. (As we shall see later, Edward I also venerated the supposed bones of King Arthur and Guinevere unearthed at Glastonbury and had them reburied in an elaborate ceremony.) Richard's wealth came from the manors, estates and castles that he held across the West Country, the Thames Valley and East Anglia, many of them rich rewards for his loyalty towards his brother (in 1264 he was to fight alongside Henry during the major rebellion of the barons under Simon de Montfort). The Earldom of Cornwall came his way quite early on in life – when he was 18 years old – and he used the wealth from this and other titles to pursue his dream of a European throne; in May 1257 he was duly crowned king of the Romans by the Pope in Rome, making him the Holy Roman Emperor, though he was unable to translate this title into real power. Richard also founded several religious houses, include Hailes Abbey in Gloucestershire, where his wife Sanchia of Provence was buried when she died in 1262, as was Richard himself when he died ten years later. In Cornwall he rebuilt Launceston, Restormel and Trematon castles – but it was Tintagel that was to be his lasting legacy.

Richard acquired the manor of Tintagel in May 1233. At that time it is likely that the only defensive fortification within his new jurisdiction was the castle at Bossiney, just under a mile to the east of Tintagel, which had been constructed by William the Conqueror's half-brother, the Earl of Mortain, soon after the Norman Conquest. Today the only visible evidence of this castle lies beside the squat Methodist church, and takes the form of a low mound cloaked in impenetrable gorse, hemlock and bracken; it's inaccessible, though clearly visible from the main road through the village, across a scruffy patch of meadowland. Bossiney is a village that is contiguous with Tintagel, though it is far less visited, partly as it is situated a little way inland from the sea. It is a quiet place with a large number of holiday homes (though very different from the 'grey, subdued village ... of scattered, humble cottages' that the writer Charles G. Harper described in his 1910 guide to the north Cornwall coast); most people just buzz through it on the road that runs along the coast. Though the castle has long gone, the mound has played a vital part in local history; it was here in November 1584 that Cornishmen raised their hands to send Francis Drake to Parliament as MP for the Borough of Bossiney – and the mound also has a walk-on part in Arthurian myth. 'According to Cornish tradition,' wrote the Revd Sabine Baring-Gould, a vicar from Devon who composed the hymn *Onward Christian Soldiers*, but was also something of a scholar on the history and folk traditions of Devon and Cornwall,

> King Arthur's golden Round Table lies deep in the earth, buried under this earthen circular mound; only on midsummer night does it rise, and then the flash of light from it for a moment illuminates the sky, after which the golden table sinks again. At the end of the world it will come to the surface again and be carried to Heaven, and the saints will sit and eat at it and Christ will serve them.

However fanciful the stories of King Arthur's Round Table resurfacing at Bossiney on midsummer night might be, no one doubts that there was once a castle there. But the situation on the promontory at Tintagel is more contentious. As we have already seen, Ralegh Radford thought that when Richard acquired the manor of Tintagel (which included Bossiney), a castle already stood on the promontory itself, built in the 1140s by Richard's predecessor as Earl of Cornwall, Reginald, who was the illegitimate son of Henry I. The presence of this earlier building is also mentioned in a number of post-war guidebooks to Tintagel. However the existence of an earlier castle from the Middle Ages on the promontory is now considered unlikely, and it is probable that by the time Richard's stonemasons arrived at Tintagel the only buildings on the promontory were those from the Dark Ages, which had by then

The lower and upper courtyards of Richard of Cornwall's castle at Tintagel. (*Andrew Beattie*)

crumbled to their foundations; however, it is possible that Richard deliberately constructed the castle on what remained of a substantial Dark Age palace, obliterating the former building in the process. If this was the case then it was a sure signal to posterity that a new generation now ruled the roost at Tintagel.

It seems probable that at the same time as the walls of his new castle were rising on the promontory, Richard had the great Iron Age ditch recut, so his castle was defended from any attackers that approached from the mainland. Above the ditch, on the tapering sliver of 'mainland' that juts towards the promontory, Richard constructed walls to enclose two courtyards, one set slightly above the other. The lower courtyard comprises a regular rectangle; the upper courtyard is more irregular in shape. The walls on the northern flanks of both courtyards directly overlooked some precipitous cliffs (and within a few decades parts of the walls had crumbled down these cliffs into the crashing sea). They are over a metre thick and their exterior would have been rendered and possibly lime-washed, making the castle appear dazzling white against the landscape. In Richard's day the interiors of these courtyards probably contained timber buildings, maybe for storage or stabling horses. Now they are just grass, though for some years a modernist sculpture of the Sword in the Stone stood in the lower (or Gatehouse) courtyard.

But it was on the adjacent promontory that Richard constructed the castle's public buildings. In those days the promontory was accessed across a narrow isthmus that was probably spanned by a stone bridge; today it is the controversial new suspension bridge that spans the void. Geoffrey of Monmouth described this isthmus as 'an access so narrow that three armed knights might hold it against the entire realm of Britain', and indeed it might be how Tintagel got its name – from the Cornish 'din' or 'tin', meaning a fortress or a natural stronghold resembling one, and 'tagell', a construction, so making 'Din Tagell', the 'Fortress of the Narrow Entrance'. It is on the promontory that the most striking medieval ruins can be found – memorable not only because of their situation, clinging to a narrow, sloping shelf of rock, but also because of their romantic, almost folly-like state of decay, the magnificent coastline serving as an appropriate backdrop in which the toothy ruins are framed.

The principal building here is the Great Hall. It is much smaller than similar halls built in the other great medieval castles of the day – though given the confines of the situation, bounded by cliff and near-vertical drop, this is perhaps to be expected. The walls are substantial, though only in one place (the former latrines) do they rise above the height of an adult; elsewhere the rocks are barely knee-high, and the shape of the Great Hall itself is confused by the remains of a later building (from the 1340s) that was constructed within its then-ruined shell. The most prominent of all the remaining medieval castle ruins are the lower frames of the windows of this original Great Hall. During the three decades or so – no more – that the Great Hall stood, Earl Richard would have dined here, his guests marvelling at the same view as today's visitors do. Arrangements were simpler than in other, larger castles; the pantry and the buttery, where food was prepared, would have been separated from the rest of the hall by no more than screens. It is thought that, in reality, Richard spent little time here; remote and isolated, his other properties near London must have been easier places where he could show off his power and wealth.

Above and right: These are the most substantial remains of Richard of Cornwall's medieval castle that can be seen today. (*Sources: Right, IDS Photos, Wikimedia Commons; above, Andrew Beattie*)

Above and below: These are the most substantial remains of Richard of Cornwall's medieval castle that can be seen today. (*Source, Lynda Poulter, Wikimedia Commons*)

Above the castle, at the promontory's highest point, are the scant remains of a chapel. Much about this building – most particularly its time of construction, and its dedicatee – remain obscure. Most sources indicate that the chapel dates from around AD 500 and was dedicated to an obscure (male) saint named Julitta, whom Ralegh Radford believed was the founder of the monastic community that once made its home on the promontory; other sources differ, however, and claim that the chapel is dedicated to Saint Juliot, an equally obscure (though this time female) Cornish saint whose martyrdom took the form of a violent death at the hands of some robbers. (Neither holy figure is to be confused with a female saint named Julitta, who was active in Tarsus in modern-day Turkey.)

The knee-high medieval ruins form the footprint of a simple building, with an entrance porch and a rectangular nave, that seems to have been grafted onto an earlier building from the Dark Ages; this building was probably a chapel, though this is by no means certain. It is possible that when he built the castle, Richard adopted this ancient place of worship as its chapel, even though it stood some distance away (castle chapels were usually built within the walls of medieval castles, not outside them). Whatever the building's history, there is not much to see now; as with all the other ruins on the island, spiky grass covers the building's interior and sprouts from much of the walls too.

Tintagel Parish Church

Somehow an ornate eleventh-century font that once graced the interior of the chapel on the promontory has now found its way to Tintagel Parish Church. This stoic building stands in remarkable isolation on the clifftop some distance away from both the village and the castle, defiant against the winter-long onslaught of wind and rain; its stolid silhouette is visible from many parts of the promontory and the mainland. The church is dedicated to the Welsh saint Materiana (or Madryn), who once ruled as a queen over Gwent and who was active as a Christian evangelist in Cornwall in the years around AD 500; her shrine was established in the church at Minster, close to Boscastle, just 5 miles along the coast from Tintagel. Minster Church is situated in a wooded dell in the valley of the River Valency and is today considered one of the most idyllically situated churches in Cornwall. The shrine of St Materiana, however, is long gone, destroyed

71

Left: The West Window of Tintagel Parish Church with the arms of Richard of Cornwall, the castle's builder, second from bottom on the right. (*Andrew Beattie*)

Below: This eleventh century font in Tintagel Parish Church formerly stood in the chapel at Tintagel Castle. (*Andrew Beattie*)

during the vandalism of the Reformation. It is likely that monks from Minster built the first priory at Tintagel, on the site of the present parish church. (Perhaps they moved between Boscastle and Tintagel via the same spectacular clifftop path that still attracts walkers to this day.) This first church at Tintagel established by the Minster monks was soon replaced by a Saxon church, which in turn was replaced by the present Norman one, established between 1080 and 1150 by the first Norman Earls of Cornwall. It was completed by Reginald, the third Earl, who was probably responsible for the church's out-of-proportion south transept (and who Ralegh Radford believed had constructed the first castle on the island).

At the west end of the church is a sturdy square tower, built in around 1400 and for centuries a landmark for sailors traversing the treacherous seas off this coast. The west window, built into its wall, depicts the history of Tintagel through heraldic shields portrayed in stained glass. The second row of designs from the bottom is the most important in the narrative of Arthur and Tintagel. On the left is the red and white shield of Robert of Mortain, the first Norman Earl of Cornwall and the builder of both Tintagel Parish Church and of Bossiney Castle, while on the right of the row the shield of Richard of Cornwall, the builder of Tintagel Castle, takes the form of a red lion surrounded by a border of black and yellow; between the two shields is the circular seal of the Borough of Bossiney. At the other end of the church is the font brought here from the castle chapel, which takes the form of a simple bowl made from a local volcanic rock known as dolerite. It has served in its time as a pig trough and a garden ornament, so understandably looks rather weather-beaten; it is housed today in an alcove in the Blessed Sacrament Chapel, a side-chapel that abuts the church's chancel. The central stone of the main altar of St Materiana is also said to have been brought from the castle chapel; the stones that flank it are twentieth century.

Tintagel from the Middle Ages to Victorian Times

Richard of Cornwall died in 1272. On his death his fantasy castle in Tintagel was upkept by his son Edmund, who died in 1300, whereupon the earldom and its estates passed to the Crown. Over the ensuing decades landslides and the weather took their toll on the castle buildings, especially the Great Hall, which in 1337 was described in a survey of the Duchy of Cornwall as 'ruinous, and its walls of no strength'. It seems that by this time the castle was in the stewardship of John of Eltham, the brother of King Edward III, who, seeing the damage already caused to the fabric of the Great Hall, ordered its roof to be dismantled. But the fortunes of the castle changed quickly, and in the 1340s further building work was undertaken, though on a much smaller scale than before. This new work consisted of a structure built within the shell of the former hall, comprising a new hall, buttery, pantry and kitchen. Today the footprint of these buildings rise little more than a few centimetres from the ground, though more substantial remains of a two-storey house (possibly a residence for the constable, or a prison) that was built at the same time can be seen on the other side of the path that leads visitors through the ruins. These buildings were constructed on the orders of Edward, Prince of Wales (also known as the Black Prince), the eldest son of King Edward III. Scant remains of further building work undertaken in the 1380s can also be seen, when the smaller hall was reduced in size, probably as a result of yet more erosion.

But it was impossible to win the battle against continuing landslips. By the fifteenth century the surviving castle buildings had been put to use as a prison, housing among others John Northampton, Lord Mayor of London, whom the Cornish antiquary and poet Richard Carew reported was incarcerated 'for his unruly mayoralty condemned thither as a perpetual penitentiary'. In 1478 the topographer William Worcester described his visit to the 'castrum de Tyntagelle', and for the first time referred to it in writing as the place both of Arthur's conception and his birth (Geoffrey of Monmouth had placed only Arthur's conception here). Not long after this, a collapse of the isthmus of land that controlled access to the castle rendered the site unusable, and dereliction set in. When the antiquarian John Leland paid a visit in 1540 he said of the place that it had been 'woren away with gulfing in of the sea, in so much that it hather made there almost an isle.' He also commented that 'the residew of the buildings of the castel be sore wetherbeten and in ruine', and provided the first mention of the castle garden, 'a grownd quadrant walled as yt were a garden plot'. Today the garden is marked by nothing more than an enclosed rectangle of grass, but Ralegh Radford excavated slabs here that might have marked out borders and flowerbeds, and it is clear that this was once the garden of the medieval castle – though its situation on a high and exposed part of the promontory is puzzling. (It has been suggested that the garden was established here – along with the chapel and a curious tunnel carved from the rock that might have served as a larder – as a 'theatrical' landscape that made direct

The antiquarian John Leland (line engraving from 1772 based on sixteenth century bust). Leland visited Tintagel in 1540 and reported on its ruinous state. (*Source: Wikimedia Commons*)

reference to the tale of Tristan and Iseult, which features a garden, along with cave or grotto in which Tristan and Iseult seek refuge.) Leland also reported that the only way onto the promontory was 'by longe elme trees layde for a bryge' across the isthmus. Even this structure seemed to have gone by 1604, however, when the cartographer John Norden came to draw the castle and labelled the gap between the promontory and the mainland as 'a draw bridge decaid'; his drawing shows a man in a red tunic climbing the 'verie steepe and craggie' cliffs to gain passage into the castle (in fact it looks as if he is actually rock climbing, so perilously vertical are the cliffs). In Norden's drawing the buildings on the mainland seem substantial, with towers and walls still intact, while those on the promontory seem in rather sorry condition, with sheep grazing among the ruins. Norden inscribed the words: 'The famous Arthur Kyng of the Brytons was here begotten in this castle' across his drawing, and lamented the disappearance of the bridge that had once linked the promontory with the mainland. Passage was now, he warned, 'far more irksome and troublesome' and that the 'tedious and dangerous' ascent to the castle was 'by a very rocky and winding way … the least slip of the foot [sending] the whole body into the devouring sea'.

Norden wrote his sorry description of Tintagel the year after James I and VI had acceded to the throne of England. The government of his predecessor, Elizabeth I, had shown no interest in Tintagel, and after the death of the last constable John Arundall in 1597, the post had been abolished. Over the next two centuries Tintagel became a forgotten curiosity. Interest in the history of England's landscapes and ancient sites grew, but Tintagel was just too remote to draw attention away from more accessible sites such as the stone circles at Stonehenge and Avebury. The old Dark Age buildings slowly sunk into the mud while much of what remained of the medieval castle of Richard of Cornwall slipped down the cliffs into the churning waters of the Atlantic. Those same cliffs still yielded useful quantities of slate, which was hewn by hand from the rocks and transported away from Tintagel by sea, as had been the case in Roman times. Copper was extracted from the natural cave beneath the castle; the miners extended and enlarged the cave and also harvested galena, a mineral ore of lead and silver, from other parts of the bay. The mining company built a small workshop and offices in the deep valley cleft that runs down to the bay, and today this squat whitewashed building serves as a café for visitors. But the castle itself languished in half-collapsed obscurity, a backdrop to the mining activities in what was then one of the most inaccessible parts of England.

Then came the great revival in medievalism of the nineteenth century. Suddenly writers and painters were keen on exploring Arthurian themes. Malory's *Morte D'Arthur* was reprinted and in 1863 the vicar of Morwenstow, a village some 20 miles northeast of Tintagel along the coast, wrote a very popular poem about the search for the Holy Grail, entitled *The Quest of the Sangraal*. The poet Swinburne also popularised Tintagel, through his poem *Iseult at Tintagel*, the action focusing on Tristan and Iseult rather than King Arthur. In the poem, Swinburne recounts how the famous love potion is drunk against a background of a storm, while a calm moment in the lovers' tempestuous relationship is marked when 'they … Saw the far sky sweep to the long grey sea / And night made one sweet mist of moor and lea … and life in them sank silent as the night.' Turner painted the castle and Tennyson's *Idylls of the King* meant Arthurian literature was more popular than ever before. And Tennyson also provided an alternative 'spin' on the legend of King Arthur's birth than the one provided by Geoffrey of Monmouth and Thomas Malory. In the *Idylls* Arthur is not conceived and born in the castle, but is instead yielded by the sea into the hands of Merlin. Tennyson recounts how Merlin,

> watched the great sea fall / Wave after wave, each mightier than the last' [in the cove beneath the castle], 'til last, a ninth one, gathering half the deep / And full of voices, slowly rose and plunged … And down the wave and in the flame was borne / A naked babe, and rode to Merlin's feet / Who stoopt and caught the babe, and cried 'The King!/Here is an heir for Uther!'

Thus the cave below the castle, which cuts right through the island from one end to the other, and which had once been hacked at by miners, came to be known as Merlin's Cave. The cave is a spectacular and magical place, partly because it curves towards the far end, meaning that it is not possible to see all the way through it; the western end opens onto a narrow beach, but as the floor of the cave is strewn with boulders and pools, and seawater invades it at high tide, passage through it is neither easy nor recommended. In February 2016 English Heritage controversially commissioned local craftsmen Peter Graham to carve a likeness of Merlin's face on the cliffside beside the cave entrance – 'official vandalism [that] diminishes our heritage', according to Kernow Matters To Us (KMTU), an organisation dedicated to preserving the integrity of Cornwall's history and culture.

The entrance to Merlin's Cave, from the cove beneath the castle. (*Andrew Beattie*)

Tourism and the Twentieth Century

Where writers and artists blazed trails, tourists soon followed – in their droves. Tintagel's champion in the Victorian era was Richard Byrn Kinsman, the vicar of Tintagel Parish Church from 1851 to 1894. He had local quarrymen cut steps cut into the cliff sides to allow for better access from the cove up to the ruins (though in 1910 the writer Charles G. Harper was still able to write that the site was accessed by 'rough, rock-cut paths, with here and there a hand rail for the timorous, [which] lead down and then up and across to the "island"'). Much improved and extended over the years, these are the same steps that today's visitors use, and find to be such a distinctive and memorable part of their visit to Tintagel. Kinsman, the very emblem of a dedicated Victorian eccentric, delighted in wearing an imposing costume of scarlet and gold as he conducted visitors around Tintagel, and in recognition of his work here, he was awarded the long-obsolete title of Constable of Tintagel by Prince Albert, head of the Duchy of Cornwall Estate. But for many years the actual keys to the castle were entrusted to a redoubtable woman named Florence Nightingale Richards, who finally retired from her position as custodian and guide aged 82 in 1938. She lived in a small dwelling known as Castle Cottage – with, for a long time, her mother – and delighted in braving the worst of storms to show visitors around the ruins.

In the 1890s it was mooted that Tintagel should be the terminus of a spur of the North Cornwall railway, which meandered through the county between Halwill Junction (on the Okehampton to Bude line) and Padstow, via Launceston and Wadebridge; the line also passed through Camelford, the nearest town to Tintagel. In 1899 a large hotel was built in Tintagel beside what would have been the station of the branch line from Camelford, and was duly named the Terminus Hotel. But the mooted link from Camelford was not to be (and the North Cornwall line itself closed in 1966, with trains on its curving, contour-hugging route unable to compete with the steadily improving roads and increased levels of car ownership). Though nothing came of the plans for a railway to Tintagel, the hotel is there to this day, built in a bombastic style that is a hybrid of Victorian Gothic and fantasy Arthuriana, its landward façade festooned with a bustling array of battlements, turrets and arrow-slit windows. It has not elicited favourable comments from writers; in his 1934 guide to Cornwall John Betjeman calls it 'conspicuous, and commanding marvellous views [but] not a pleasant addition to the landscape'. These days it's called the Camelot Castle Hotel and stands sentinel on the next headland along

The Camelot Castle Hotel, built on the cliffs near the castle in the early twentieth century in a hybrid of Victorian Gothic and fantasy Arthurian styles. (*Andrew Beattie*)

from the castle, visible for miles around. Since its opening it has attracted luminaries – in 1923 Sir Edward Elgar composed the incidental music of Laurence Binyon's play *Arthur* while staying as a guest at the hotel – but he, like everyone else who visited Tintagel, had to make the last part of his long journey here by road from the railway station at Camelford (which itself was 2 miles from the town it served, lost in the middle of nowhere). Later, films such as the 1953 MGM epic *Knights of the Round Table* staring Ava Gardner as Guinevere (and utilising some Tintagel residents as extras), and 1979's *Dracula*, staring Laurence Olivier, were filmed at the hotel. Today it's the hotel's restored drawing room that draws the eye, with its enormous fireplace, marble pillars, heavy curtains, Arthurian memorabilia (including, of course, a round table), grand piano, well-worn sofas and picture windows overlooking the sea; the whole ensemble is like something out of a bygone age, of chivalry, perhaps, or at least Edwardian gentility. The restoration is the work of its current owners (thankfully the place has not fallen into the hands of a bland international hotel chain), who are John Mappin of the diamond and jewellery empire Mappin and Webb, along with his wife Irina and the artist Ted Stourton, whose work adorns many of the walls. They have imbued the place with a sense of character and individualism throughout, which makes the hotel one of the most memorable places to stay in the whole of Cornwall.

By the time the hotel opened, Tintagel was already heaving with visitors in the busy summer months. In 1910 Charles G. Harper lamented that 'no latter-day traveller coming to Tintagel can fail to be disappointed with it. Let the hopeful pilgrim to the chief shrine of the Arthurian legend reconcile himself to bitter disenchantment.' (He condemns the Terminus Hotel as a 'recent hideous bulk' that only manages to look 'romantic rather than vulgar' on the occasions that it is partially obscured by a descending sea mist.) He went on to complain that 'a very sorry change' wrought by 'Tennyson's picture of the place and of King Arthur' had come about since the time when 'the village still remained Travena [when] it was a place of a few scattered cottages … of the Cornish kind.' (The village had changed its name from Travena to Tintagel to help boost tourism.) He was concerned, too, that the venerable seventeenth-century building that once housed the post office 'might be demolished, in order to clear the ground for villas and boarding houses of the horrific type that now sears the soul of the sentimental traveller in these parts.' In actual fact he had nothing to fear on this score; the building remains, a sight for visitors to tick off after they have toured the castle and the Hall of Chivalry. But

Harper was clear as to who was to blame for the situation. 'Tennyson is responsible for this, for King Arthur and Tintagel had not become a cult before he wrote *Idylls of the King*.' He went on to admit that he believed,

> in King Arthur, not necessarily by that name, but [it appears beyond doubt] that there was a historical, or, if you like it better, a prehistoric personage on whom the great figure of Arthur is based. But I decline to believe he in any way resembled the person Tennyson pictures, with the manner of a Sunday School teacher, and language to match. The school-marms, university-extensionists, and spectacled professorial persons, whom we see walking Tintagel and the country round about, with the Tennysonian Arthur in their minds, would not, one shrewdly suspects, have liked the real Arthur, who was probably a man of wrath and blood, full of patriotic sentiments, but giving expression to them rather with the sword than by word of mouth. I am quite sure the affectionate maiden aunts who present good nephews with *Idylls of the King,* hoping the recipients will take the Tennysonian hero for a model, would be quite horrified could they know the real Arthur.

The poet, playwright and opera librettist Ronald Duncan was another noted figure who bemoaned the commercialisation of Tintagel and the shameless exploitation of the fascination with King Arthur. 'At Tintagel we see nothing now but the commercial exploitation of these myths,' he wrote in his 1966 guide to Devon and Cornwall. 'It is the achievement of the twentieth century to turn a poem into a bazaar; Isolde into an ashtray.' And that was all he said about the place – along the north Cornwall coast, Delabole slate quarry and Penfound Manor, a stately home at Poundstock, near Bude, were much more successful at commanding his attention. John Betjeman, legendary lover of Cornwall, was kinder to Tintagel in his *Shell Guide* to the county, one of a series of travel guides for motorists that were published throughout the 1930s to cover much of Britain and 'sponsored by Shell-Mex and BP Ltd'. In the guide Betjeman extols the savage beauty of Cornish seascapes and the tranquillity of its country churches – and at Tintagel he is stirred by the 'black jagged slate of which the Norman castle is built, the loop holes for arrows, the mighty inaccessible cliffs of black slate' that visitors would encounter, along with the 'ever present merciless roll of the heaving Atlantic, [which] all lend strength to the legend [of King Arthur]'. In his later guide, published in 1964, Betjeman had tired of the tourists, and commented that,

> This slaty sea coast parish is best seen out of season and on a stormy day. Then the windswept uplands, treeless and barren, by which it is approached have their true quality of storm-resisting loneliness. The gift shops in the village ... seem flimsier and more futile; the car parks are mostly wind whipped ponds.

It is a shame that in all the extraordinary poetry Betjeman wrote about Cornwall, Tintagel never featured; instead, he was drawn to locations 10 miles further along the coast, around Trebetherick and Polzeath, across the Camel estuary from Padstow. But he did write some memorable lines about travelling on the North Cornwall Railway to Padstow, the place of childhood holidays lovingly recalled in his nostalgic verse autobiography *Summoned by Bells*:

> The emptying train, wind in the ventilators, / Puffs out of Egloskerry to Tresmeer [two stops before Camelford] ... Can it really be that this same carriage came from Waterloo? / On Wadebridge's platform what a breath of sea scented the Camel valley! / Soft air, soft Cornish rains, and silence after steam.

In 1929 the Duchy of Cornwall estate, faced with the competing pressures to preserve Tintagel, but also to open it up to both tourists and archaeologists, placed the castle in the hands of the government's Office of Works (though Florence Nightingale Richards would continue to guide people around the site for another ten years). By the 1970s Cornwall's beach resorts were heaving throughout the summer with carloads of holidaymakers, and Tintagel was an increasingly popular day trip for families with young children. The steps that were draped up and over the site like necklaces were deemed to be too worn and steep to be safe, so a bridge was built to breach the steepest flights of steps, which led up and down the chasm that separated the promontory from the mainland. This bridge in turn was replaced by a spectacular new pedestrian steel suspension bridge which opened in the summer of 2019, whose design – sleek and elegant though it undoubtedly is – has brought criticism from many quarters.

And still, the legend of Arthur clings to this place as tenaciously as the ruins of Richard of Cornwall's castle cling to the slopes above the cove.

The new pedestrian suspension bridge. (*Source, English Heritage*)

In 1998 the community of Arthur enthusiasts was briefly excited by the discovery of the so-called 'Arthur stone', or more formally the Artognou Slate, a thin slab of rock that had been broken to fit over a Dark Age drain and on which fragments of script were written. These fragments seemed to include the word 'Artognou', a sixth-century Celtic name similar in origin to the name 'Arthur', and which can be translated as 'bear-like'; the image of a bear was used in early poetry to represent heroic valour, as was the name 'Art' or 'Arthur', though attempts to portray this as proof positive that Tintagel at last had an evidential link with King Arthur soon crumbled away like those Cornish cliffs that drop away from the old walls of the castle, when it was realised that in the sixth century 'Arthur' would have been written as 'Artorius', rather than 'Artognou'. Other words on the stone include 'ficit' – he made – and it is possible, as evidenced by the casual style of the writing and the repetitive nature of the letters, that this was merely the work of a stone cutter practising his letter-carving (similar to the stone found more recently, during the archaeological digs of 2017). The stone offers no proof of Arthur's existence (though it does suggest that the castle has yet to yield up all its secrets). Sceptics and believers alike can examine the stone for themselves in the Royal Cornwall Museum in Truro, where it's displayed along with the other Tintagel finds; it's smaller than might be

Above: Tintagel is one of the most popular tourist villages in Cornwall. (*Andrew Beattie*)

Left: One of the many reminders of Tintagel's Arthurian heritage - the King Arthur's Arms pub. (*Andrew Beattie*)

The so-called 'Arthur Stone' (or Artognou Slate) on display in the Royal Cornwall Museum in Truro. (*Andrew Beattie*)

expected, just thirty centimetres or so across, but some of the scratchings on it, including the letter 'A' of 'Artognou' with its classically Celtic downward-pointing bar, seem fresh enough to have been carved yesterday.

The Hall of Chivalry

Tintagel's final Arthurian flourish – and the most enduring mark the twentieth century has made on the place – comes in the form of a piece of high kitsch that was established in the centre of the village in the early 1930s by, of all people, a man who had earned himself a fortune from manufacturing custard powder. Frederick Thomas Glasscock was a founding partner in the firm of Monkhouse and Glasscock, which was based in Clerkenwell in North London. As well as selling mountains of custard powder, the firm also developed the cake decoration known as 'hundreds and thousands' (the firm was eventually bought out by Bird's Custard in 1958; Glasscock's business partner was the grandfather of the comedian Bob Monkhouse). On retiring from the custard and cake-decoration business Glasscock decided to move to Cornwall. But millionaire custard-powder manufacturers are not the sort to spend their retirement in Cornwall happily tending to the garden of their thatched cottage. Soon after he arrived in the county Glasscock found himself intoxicated by the mysticism of King Arthur, and decided to glorify the legendary king (and in many ways, himself) by constructing the so-called Hall of Chivalry, a set of two extravagantly decorated halls packed with Arthuriana that sit behind the frontage of a fairly ordinary looking house that overlooks the main T-junction in Tintagel village. Here, Glasscock was determined, in his words, 'to perpetuate Arthur's ideals of chivalry'. Today the place is popular year-round with visitors, who come to marvel at Glasscock's creation and maybe to buy themselves into his Fellowship of the Order of the Knights of the Round Table, which was revived in 1993 (benefits of joining include a numbered membership card, a lapel badge, a CD of the actor Robert Powell telling the story of King Arthur's Halls, and a quarterly newsletter). The Hall is now owned by the Freemasons, who use it for various ceremonies – as do their associated order, the Knights Templar Association.

From the start, Glasscock's offering of a 'Fellowship' for his pseudo chivalric order served variously as a gimmick to pull in visitors, a fundraising exercise and an easy way by which Glasscock could indulge in his Arthurian fantasies. When he established the fellowship in the 1930s a child could join as a 'searcher', a teenager would be a 'pilgrim', while an adult would be a 'knight' (and all would have to be proposed and seconded before they secured membership). The elaborate initiation ceremonies included attendants wearing an array of different colours to denote their rank and status, the principles of the order being read from a scroll, and Glasscock, (in the role of Arthur) drawing Excalibur from a scabbard and striking the new member of the Fellowship on the shoulder, naming him Sir Galahad, Bedivere or Lancelot, as appropriate. From 1929, when the first hall opened, the business snowballed and it was clear that a new, grander hall was needed. This was duly constructed beyond the original hall, and on 5 June 1933 over 500 people packed the grand opening ceremony, including the Bishop of Truro, who consecrated the building (hence its use as a venue for weddings). Buoyed by his success, Glasscock proved benevolent in other ways, endowing Tintagel with tennis courts, a men's club and the establishment of facilities for scouts and guides. Glasscock established branches of his fellowship in New South Wales and Boston, and in the 1930s membership of his organisation numbered 17,000. Sadly he died a year after the second hall was opened, in July 1934, returning from a fundraising trip to the United States on the Cunard liner, *Scythia*; he was buried at sea.

Splendidly over-the-top, the Hall of Chivalry does at least provide a vivid introduction to the Arthur myth for children – though for adults the insistence at Arthurian initiation ceremonies on period costumes, solemn ritual and arcane language lends the place an atmosphere than can be hard to pin down. Today a visit begins in the darkened smaller hall where, with

Above and below: The Halls of Chivalry at Tintagel are the work of a millionnaire Arthur enthusiast and celebrated Arthurian, Frederick Glasscock. (*Andrew Beattie*)

the aid of lights, a booming commentary by Merlin (actually Robert Powell) tells the history of the halls and of Arthur. From here visitors proceed into the larger, newer hall beyond, for an immersion in Arthuriana that can last as long as they like. The way to make sense of the place is to remember that what Glasscock was getting at here was his own version of the medieval Order of the Round Table. This knightly order was established in 1344 by King Edward III, 'in the same manner and condition as Arthur, formerly king of England, established it', according to the English historian Adam Murimuth, who was King Edward's contemporary. Edward's medieval order did not last long, however. Although a new building was begun at Windsor Castle to house a Round Table, the king lost interest and founded another chivalric order instead that consisted of himself, the Prince of Wales and twenty-four knights. This was the Order of the Garter, which proved rather more enduring, and today is one of the most famous of all ceremonial orders. So in many ways Glasscock's kitschy creation easily eclipses King Edward's first attempt at a chivalric order. Nearly a hundred years after his Order's foundation it is still possible to become a member, while Edward III's Arthurian foundation fizzled and died within just a few years.

Chapter Two

The Quest for Camelot

Winchester, Caerleon, Caerwent and Cadbury Castle

Most people have an image of Camelot, King Arthur's fabled court, in their mind's eye; it is a fairy-tale fortress of gap-tooth battlements and conical turrets that reach upwards into the dreamy heavens, and it is surrounded by a veritable arcadia of gardens, rivers and forests. The Camelot dreamed up by Mark Twain in his 1889 novel *A Connecticut Yankee in King Arthur's Court* fits the bill exactly: 'a far-away town sleeping in a valley by a winding river,' is how Twain's hero, the 'yankee', first encounters Camelot; 'beyond it on a hill [was] a vast grey fortress, with towers and turrets.' An earlier description of Camelot in literature comes in Alfred, Lord Tennyson's poem *Gareth and Lynette*, published in 1872 and part of his epic verse cycle *Idylls of the King*. When the poem's hero Gareth first approaches Arthur's fortress, desperate to become a knight, he encounters a place of magic and fantasy, a 'Royal mount / That rose between the forest and the field. / At times the summit of the high city flashed; / At times the spires and turrets half-way down / Pricked through the mist.' This later becomes the arena in which Gareth pursues the beautiful Lynette – through a 'city of Enchanters, built / By fairy Kings ... a city of shadowy palaces / And stately, rich in emblem and the work / Of ancient kings who did their days in stone'. Tennyson offers an even more iconic description of Camelot in another poem, *The Lady of Shalott*. This lyrical ballad tells the story (derived from a tale from the Vulgate Cycle) of a young woman imprisoned on an island who will be cursed if she looks directly at the 'many-tower'd Camelot' that is surrounded by 'long fields of barley and of rye / That clothe the world and meet the sky'. Eventually the lady dies of unrequited love for Lancelot, and at Camelot 'Knight and burgher, lord and dame' gather on the castle quayside to watch as the boat carrying her body drifts into view, prompting Lancelot to sigh that 'She has a lovely face / God in his mercy lend her grace, The Lady of Shalott.'

But did this fantastical palace of King Arthur and his knights of the Round Table ever actually exist? And if it did, where was it located? Tennyson wrote parts of *Idylls of the King* in the small town of Caerleon in South Wales, a former Roman military encampment that is one of many 'contenders' for the location of Arthur's fantastical

Camelot as depicted by Gustave Doré in an 1868 edition of Tennyson's *Idylls of the King.* (*Source, Wikimedia Commons*)

court. But every author who has written about Camelot – going back to the Middle Ages – has placed it in a different location on the map, with the result that the 'quest' for Camelot has led historians and 'Arthur' enthusiasts to a variety of places across Wales, northern England, Cornwall and the West Country in their search for Arthur's fabled fortress. Their quest is most likely futile; most scholars regard Camelot as being entirely fictional – among them Norris J. Lacy, an American academic who specialises in Arthurian literature, who has reached the conclusion that 'Camelot, located nowhere in particular, can be anywhere.' Nevertheless, arguments about the location of the 'real Camelot' have raged since the fifteenth century, and continue to this day, often for the purposes of attracting tourists ('Come to our town, home to King Arthur's Camelot!'). Yet if King Arthur himself is, at best, a shadowy and elusive presence, then his mythical castle is even more so.

Camelot in Early Arthurian Literature

Camelot is absent from the early Arthurian stories – though that is not to say that in these narratives Arthur did not have a glorious court. Geoffrey of Monmouth places this at Caerleon, near Newport in Southeast Wales, and his descriptions drew on an already established tradition that told of its grandeur. This tradition had an early voice in the Welsh tale *Culhwch and Olwen*, associated with the cycle of stories known as the *Mabinogion* and probably written in the eleventh century. In this tale we are told that powerful warriors gathered at King Arthur's court before embarking on their great adventures. This court has a name – Celliwig – which has been identified with an Iron Age hill-fort in Cornwall named the Kelly Rounds (also known as castle Killibury), situated just outside the town of Wadebridge, close to the section of the A39 trunk road dubbed (by tourism chiefs no doubt) the 'Atlantic Highway'. Unfortunately there is nothing to detain tourists at this bleak and uninspiring spot (accessed by a minor road that leads off the A39, but not even given the honour of a signpost from it); only a semicircle of shallow earthworks remain (the rest are obliterated by an ungainly cluster of modern farm buildings on the other side of a minor road) and these ditches and banks are overgrown with a tangle of brambles and trees. No one has thought to put up any information boards, or even a sign. In fact the Kelly Rounds are the least inspiring of all the Camelot contenders, and more absorbing than visiting the site is an examination of King Arthur's court as described in *Culhwch and Olwen*. In the tale the hero Culhwch, who is Arthur's cousin and is infatuated with the giant's daughter Olwen, has difficulty gaining entrance to the palace while a feast is in progress. Though there is no description of the place, the implications of the story are that Celliwig is a place of great opulence, wealth and splendour. There is also, apparently, a spectacular view. 'From here,' we are assured, 'one of Arthur's warriors, Drem, could see a gnat as far away as Scotland, while another, Medyr, could shoot an arrow through the legs of a wren in Ireland!' Kelly Rounds is located on a level, broad, low rise and has no view to speak of – though other contenders for Celliwig may do better in that department (they include the market town of Callington in Southeast Cornwall, the small village of Kelly close to the River Tamar in Devon, and a farm named Gelliweg on the Llyn Peninsula in Gwynedd). The thirteenth-century Welsh Triads also locate one of Arthur's courts at Celliwig, but in contrast to *Culhwch and Olwen*, these tales maintain that Arthur had multiple courts, with others situated in Wales and northern England.

The first author to mention Camelot by name was Chrétien de Troyes, in his poem *Lancelot*. This was written in the 1170s as a reworking of the tale of Guinevere's abduction that had originally been told by Caradoc of Llancarfan in his *Life of Gildas* a few decades earlier. However, Arthur's court is mentioned by Chrétien only in passing, with the appearance of Camelot left to the reader's imagination. 'A un jor d'une Acenssion / Fu venuz de vers Carlion / Li rois Artus et tenu ot / Cort molt riche a Camaalot, / Si riche com au jor estut,' Chrétien tells us; 'King Arthur, one Ascension Day, was in the region near Caerleon and held a most magnificent court at Camelot with all the splendour as befitted a king.'

So Chrétien followed Geoffrey's lead and placed Arthur's court at Caerleon. But from where did Chrétien derive the name of his fabulous castle? For all the academic discussion that this evocative name has prompted, it seems probable that he simply made it up, for there is no trace of it in any other sources or local tradition. Was the name of the site of Arthur's final battle, Camlann, the inspiration? The two place names are certainly similar. Other suggestions abound; perhaps 'Camelot' has its origins in a corruption of Avalon, Arthur's final resting place, and Caerleon; on the other hand, the 'lot' part of the word may derive from the French word for 'portion' or 'fate' and it has been suggested that Chrétien possibly chose it so that Camelot would rhyme with 'tenue ot' in the previous line of the poem. Then again, it is also interesting to note that in some very early versions of Chrétien's work Camelot is not mentioned at all, and instead Arthur is said to hold court 'con lui plot', meaning 'as he pleased', which might then have been rendered as 'Camelot' in future editions (possibly even by careless scribes). Whatever the case, the word quickly entered the lexicon of Arthuriana, though in medieval French romances it has a number of spelling, including Camaalot, Camalot, Chamalot, Camehelot, Camchilot, Camaaloth, Caamalot, Camahaloth, Camaelot, Kamaalot, Kamaaloth, Kaamalot, Kamahaloth, Kameloth, Kamaelot, Kamelot, Kaamelot, Cameloth, Camelot and Gamalaot.

Nothing in Chrétien's poem suggests the level of importance Camelot would have in later Arthurian romances. In fact like Geoffrey of Monmouth before him, Chrétien depicts Arthur holding court at a number of cities and castles, as was the typical practice of medieval monarchs. It is not until the French prose romances of the late thirteenth century (the Vulgate Cycle) that Camelot began to be described as Arthur's principal and most glorious court. As this cycle of poems developed, so the descriptions of Camelot became ever more lavish. Poets described the town as being surrounded by forests and meadows with open space for knightly tournaments. The Vulgate Cycle's *Story of Merlin* describes Camelot as a 'rich and well provided town' but offers few details as to its layout or exact size. However, it was small enough that during a particularly busy gathering so many barons and nobles came that 'not a tenth of them could be lodged in the city of Camelot, and the others found shelter in the meadowland, which was wide and beautiful, in tents and pavilions.' The city's defences were formidable; at one point a group of knights climbed onto the walls to see whether or not the Saxon hordes were approaching the city. Within the city Arthur held court in a castle furnished with courtyards, bedrooms, areas for feasting and, apparently, the Round Table, and it was close enough to a body of water for the king to see a boat approaching bearing a dead maiden. None of these stories hint at where Camelot might actually be located. But Camelot's imprecise geography serves the romances well, and soon the fabled castle had become less a literal place than a powerful symbol of Arthur's court and universe – though it was always more celebrated by French writers than English ones, who, with the exception of the anonymous poet who wrote

Sir Gawain and the Green Knight and named Arthur's court as being at Camelot, followed the tradition of Geoffrey of Monmouth and favoured locating his court at Caerleon.

Winchester: Thomas Malory's Camelot

All this changed in the late fifteenth-century, when Sir Thomas Malory located Camelot at the city of Winchester in Southern England in his epic work *Le Morte d'Arthur*. The identification comes right at the end of Book Two, much of which is concerned with the exploits of Balin le Savage, 'the knight with two swords', who is killed by his brother Balan in a fight where both are disguised and neither is aware of who the other is. Balan also dies in the fight and Merlin has the brothers buried in the same tomb. Malory describes how 'Merlin let make by his subtlety that Balin's sword was put in a marble stone standing upright as great as a mill stone, and the stone hovered always above the water and did many years.' The stone then seems to develop a magical life of its own, as,

> by adventure it swam down the stream to the City of Camelot, that is in English, Winchester. And that same day Galahad the haut prince came with King Arthur, and so Galahad brought with him the scabbard and achieved the sword that was there in the marble stone hoving upon the water.

When Malory wrote *Morte d'Arthur* the identification of Winchester as Camelot was already ingrained into the popular tradition of medieval England. The year before the work appeared, King Henry VII had made sure that his first-born son – a new hope, the living example of the reconciliation of the houses of York and Lancaster at the end of the Wars of the Roses – was called Arthur and, moreover, was born in Winchester. Henry, who had defeated Richard III at Bosworth Field just a year before his son was born, had a weak claim to the throne, having descended through an illegitimate Lancastrian line that could be traced back to John of Gaunt, the son of Edward III. He was also Welsh – something that might have been a drawback to his ruling England. But once on the throne he set about trying to prove that through his Welsh ancestors he was descended from King Arthur; and he was determined that his son and heir would be that king reborn, in name and in birthplace. Immediately after his birth at St Swithun's Priory, the monastery attached to Winchester Cathedral, young Arthur was christened in the cathedral and was then sent to be raised at Ludlow Castle in the Welsh Marches. Here, at the age of 5, he was anointed Prince of Wales, and at the age of 11 he was formally betrothed to the Spanish princess Catherine of Aragon, whom he married on his fifteenth birthday. For a time it looked as if when Henry died he would be succeeded by a 'real' King Arthur. But this was not to be; tragedy struck soon after the marriage, and Arthur died at Ludlow, leaving his younger brother Henry (who acceded as Henry VIII) as the heir to the throne. Yet despite Prince Arthur's early death, the Arthurian theme was to play an important part in the mythology of the Tudor dynasty, with both Henry VIII and Elizabeth I commissioning and attending pageants and plays celebrating the fabled king from which all Tudors claimed descent.

It is difficult to identify exactly when the tradition identifying Winchester as Camelot first arose. (The identification remained popular for centuries, though it was rejected by Malory's own editor, William Caxton, who preferred a Welsh location for Camelot.) In Geoffrey of

Henry VII's son Arthur, Prince of Wales, depicted (right) on a Victorian stained glass window at St Lawrence's Church in Ludlow, Shropshire, where he died. He was the nephew of Edward Plantagenet (left), one of the two Princes in the Tower. (*Andrew Beattie*)

Monmouth's *Historia*, Winchester is described as the location for the court of Uther Pendragon, Arthur's father, though not of Arthur himself. Geoffrey also features the city in other parts of his work; after the death of Arthur, for example, he tells how the son of the defeated Mordred joins forces with the Saxons to fight Arthur's successor Constantine – though without success, and when defeat seems imminent one of the brothers eventually ends up holing himself up in Winchester.

That the city features in Geoffrey's work is partly down to its long and venerable history. Winchester was a prominent urban centre throughout Celtic, Roman and Saxon times. Its cathedral was founded in the 660s and two centuries later King Alfred the Great ruled his Kingdom of Wessex from here. Under King Canute (1016–35) Winchester became the centre of royal power and administration and the *de facto* capital of England. By the time Malory wrote *Morte d'Arthur* the city was no longer England's capital – the Normans had bestowed that honour on London – but it was nonetheless home to two institutions of national importance. They were a magnificent new Gothic cathedral, constructed from 1079 onwards, and a venerable school, namely Winchester College, founded in 1382 and today one of the most prestigious schools in England. The College even plays a part in the King Arthur story, for it was here in 1934 that the then Headmaster, W. F. Oakeshott, discovered a previously unknown manuscript copy of *Morte d'Arthur* during the cataloguing of the college's library. Oakeshott later wrote that the later edition prepared by Caxton showed 'startling evidence of revision' when compared with the older handwritten edition that had been unearthed – though microscopic examination of ink smudges on the pages have suggested that the Winchester manuscript was at one time in the possession of Caxton's printing workshop. But in the Middle Ages the cathedral and the nearby school played no part in Winchester's identification with King Arthur; that link came about because of an extraordinary artefact that hung in the Great Hall of Winchester Castle – and which still hangs there today. The artefact in question was none other than the legendary Round Table, the glorious centrepiece of King Arthur's court.

Winchester's Round Table

Winchester is a city of dreamy riverside walks and handsome streets of pastel and flint that cluster around the extraordinary and vast cathedral, whose nave is the longest of any Gothic church in Europe, and whose deceased incumbents include Jane Austen, King Canute and William Rufus, the son and successor of William the Conqueror. (Beside the cathedral is a fine historical museum, spread over several floors of a handsome townhouse – though it has nothing to say about King Arthur, Thomas Malory or Camelot.) Such is the draw of the city centre that the Great Hall of Winchester Castle is easily overlooked by visitors. This cavernous space is located not in the city centre but on a rise overlooking it – a stroll of five minutes or so from the High Street, through the West Gate, one of the remaining fortified entrances to the city that date from the Middle Ages. The castle was founded in 1067, one of many built across England by the Normans to strike fear and awe into the subjects of their newly conquered land. In the early twelfth century a great stone keep was added, and the 'pipe rolls' of the Exchequer from 1155 show that there was a 'complex of halls, chambers and chapels which constituted a medieval palace.' The castle's heyday, however, came during the long reign of Henry III, who was born in the castle in 1207, the eldest son of King John. We know little about Henry's childhood at Winchester beyond the fact that in 1212, when he was 5 years old, his education was entrusted to Peter des Roches, the Bishop of Winchester – a Frenchman, like many bishops of Norman England, whose tomb can still be seen in the cathedral. The other thing we know about Henry's childhood was that it was cut short, as he became king in 1216, at the age of just 9. England was wracked by civil war at the time, which meant young Henry had to be crowned in Gloucester Cathedral, rather than Westminster Abbey, and when Peter des Roches crowned him it was with a simple gold corolla, the traditional crown having been lost during the political upheavals.

During Henry's minority rule the political situation in England stabilised and in 1222, when he was still a young teenager, Henry was able to order the construction of his showpiece Great Hall at Winchester Castle. This magnificent space (built on the site of the Great Hall of the Norman castle) was built to a 'double cube' design, measuring 110 ft by 55 ft by 55 ft, fashioned from flint with stone dressings, and divided (not unlike a three-aisled basilica) by marble pillars into a central 'nave' flanked by side aisles. But it was only to serve the castle for a few decades. In 1302, some eighty years after construction work began on the hall, the castle's royal apartments were destroyed by fire; the king, Edward I (Henry's son), and his queen were asleep in their chambers when the fire broke out. They managed to escape but the royal apartments were too badly damaged to rebuild, and survived as a ruin, eventually to be demolished on the orders of Oliver Cromwell in 1649. The Great Hall, however, was intact and was spared the attention of the demolition mallets. Today the hall – whose adjacent long gallery houses a small museum on the history of the hall and its famous table – is all that remains of the castle, although across a paved forecourt in front of it are some sunken ruins of some of the castle buildings that have been unearthed during archaeological digs.

This forecourt is approached along Castle Avenue, all cobbles and elegant medieval-looking buildings with extravagant oriel windows; but the whole ensemble along Castle Avenue dates from the 1890s – and was, apparently, the first piece of formal town planning in Winchester since Alfred the Great laid out the street system in the ninth century. The medieval-style garden behind the Great Hall, called Queen Eleanor's Garden, is also a piece of faux-medieval whimsy, created in 1986, and the buildings that surround the Hall today are of a variety of styles, from pseudo-medieval to wholly undistinguished sixties functionalism. These buildings serve as various administrative offices of Hampshire County Council, along with Winchester Crown Court, which is housed within a 1970s building adjacent to the Hall. But the Hall itself has served as a courthouse on a number of occasions. One of the earliest trials held here was in 1330, when Edmund of Woodstock, First Earl of Kent, was tried for fomenting rebellion against Edward III. Subsequent trials include the 1603 trial of Sir Walter Raleigh and two others who were found guilty of plotting to overthrow James I (they were reprieved at the last moment even as scaffolds were being erected outside); the 1685 trial of Lady Alice Lisle, who was condemned to death by 'hanging' Judge Jeffreys for harbouring two fugitives from the Monmouth rebellion; and the November 1973 IRA trial which saw two women and six men found guilty for planting car bombs outside the Old Bailey and Scotland Yard in March of the same year. Although the Great Hall's days as a court house now seem to be behind it – the long gallery and gift shop occupy the former Jury Rooms – the administrative role played by the buildings in this part of the city continues. But it has to be said that Winchester's best days – when the whole of England was run from here – are behind it; nowadays the city has to make do with just running Hampshire.

As for the Round Table, it's the Hall's focus and draw; everything else – the surprising airiness of the space, the contrast between the rough stone walls and the smooth marble of the pillars, the nineteenth-century windows with their armorial shields of Hampshire worthies picked out in stained glass – shrinks away in deference to the artefact that everyone has come to see. The table hangs high on the wall at one end of the hall and looks for all the world like an enormous dart board, the centre occupied by a red 'bullseye' (which turns into a Tudor Rose up close) and the segments splaying away from it picked out alternatively in green and cream. In the Middle Ages it was widely believed to be the genuine table around which King Arthur had sat with his knights – hence Malory's and Henry VII's choice of Winchester as Camelot. But it is, in fact, a work of medieval fakery, probably constructed for a royal feast during the reign of Winchester's own Henry III, whose extraordinarily long reign was to last until 1272 – though other sources claim that the table was built later, in 1290, for an Arthurian tournament to celebrate the marriages of the children of Edward I in April of that year. The table has a diameter of twenty feet, weighs around 2,600lbs and is made from 121 separate pieces of English oak. During renovation work in 1976 the table was taken down from the wall and examined; tree-ring analysis indicated that wood from

The Great Hall of Winchester Castle, in which the famous Winchester Round Table is housed. (*Source, John Bakker, Wikimedia Commons*)

Above and left: The Round Table in the former Great Hall of Winchester Castle. (*Andrew Beattie*)

seven oak trees was used for the construction of the table, and carbon dating indicates that these trees were felled some time between 1236 and 1319. The mortice holes into which the legs fitted when the table stood upright were also clearly visible. It was also discovered that all the painting on the table dates to the early sixteenth century, and that when the table was originally constructed it was just bare wood. The designs are all thought to have been ordered by Henry VIII, who continued his father's obsession with the Tudor line having descended from a Welsh King Arthur. Along with the Tudor rose, the designs include the names of twenty-four of Arthur's knights around the circumference, and a depiction of a resplendent bearded and crowned King Arthur himself. Henry made his first visit to Winchester as king in 1516 and within days he had issued a writ for 'the repair of the Great Hall at Winchester and the Round Table there'. In 1522 Henry brought the Holy Roman Emperor Charles V to Winchester to show off the glorious new table, and X-ray analysis has shown that at that time King Arthur's face closely resembled that of King Henry – a deliberate gesture that would remind Charles of the inheritance of the British kings and their descent from King Arthur (though repainting over the centuries has aged the figure and has rendered the resemblance less clear). The table has hung on the west wall of the Great Hall since it was moved in 1873 from the east wall – where it had possibly been hanging since the time of Henry III or Edward I. It is the single most venerated object of Arthuriana anywhere, and has been drawing the eyes of everyone from the Arthur-obsessed to the merely curious since the Middle Ages.

The earliest appearance of the Round Table in written texts comes in the works of the Anglo-Norman poet Maistre Wace, whose poem *Roman de Brut*, written in around 1155, relates how Arthur's barons could not agree on precedence in seating at court. The problem was that

> each one believed himself to be the best, and no one could tell the worst, [so] King Arthur ... established the Round Table. There sat the vassals, all of them at the table-head, and all equal ... none of them could boast that he was seated higher than his peer.

Wace originally had the king sit at a separate table on a dais, though in later adaptations Arthur joins his knights at the table. The legend of the

Round Table was embellished by Layamon, a priest and poet from the Worcestershire village of Areley Kings whose poem *Brut* (also known as the *Chronicle of Britain*) was written in around 1190, in Middle English (it was translated into English prose in 1847 by Sir Frederick Madden). Layamon claims that the table has its origins during an argument at a Christmas banquet when there was a quarrel over knightly precedence; Arthur had the knight who started the quarrel beheaded, along with his kinsmen, while the knight's female kin had their noses cut off. But the notion of precedence had clearly troubled Arthur. A solution to the problem was offered to him on a later trip to Cornwall, where he met a carpenter – a 'crafty workman' in Madden's translation – who offered to build him a table that could seat 1,600 men yet be carried anywhere. 'I am thine own man,' the workman assured him,

> I know of tree-works wondrous many crafts … I will thee work a board [table] exceeding fair, that thereat may sit sixteen hundred and more, all turn about, so that none be without; without and within, man against man. And when thou wilt, after thy will; and then thou needest never fear, to the world's end, that ever any moody knight at the board and make fight, for there shall the high be even with the low.

The enthusiastic workman was supplied with timber, and work duly begun.

> At a high day the folk was assembled, and Arthur himself approached soon to the board, and ordered all his knights to the board forthright. When all were seated, knights to their meat, then spake each with other; as if it were his brother … every sort of knight was there exceeding well disposed; all they were one by one seated, the high and the low.

It is clear that within a century of Maistre Wace's work the Round Table was playing such an intrinsic part in the Arthur stories that Henry III or Edward I felt moved enough to build the great table that can still be seen today in Winchester. Yet Wace clearly stated he was not the source of the Round Table legend, and both he and Layamon maintained that the object had appeared earlier in Breton tales. But these tales – if they ever existed – are now lost, and may themselves derive from a custom recorded in Celtic stories in which warriors sit in a circle around the king or lead warrior, in some cases feuding over the order of precedence, as they do in Layamon's narrative. And some scholars have suggested an even earlier origin for the legend of the Round Table. In two biographies of Charlemagne, Einhard's *Vita Caroli Magni* (written sometime between 817 and 830) and Notker the Stammerer's *De Carolo Magno* (written in the 880s), the emperor is described as owning a round table with a map of Rome depicted at its centre – a possible prototype for the one later said to be in the possession of King Arthur.

King Arthur's Round Table as depicted by Évrard d'Espinques, a French manuscript illuminator active between 1440 and 1494. (*Source, Wikimedia Commons*)

Whatever the source of the legend, King Arthur's Round Table took on a different dimension in the Vulgate Cycle, the French romances composed during the late twelfth and early thirteenth century. In Robert de Boron's *Merlin*, written (like Layamon's *Brut*) in the 1190s, the Round Table is created by Merlin in imitation of the table that Christ's disciples sat at on the occasion of the Last Supper; Merlin creates the table for Arthur's father Uther Pendragon rather than for Arthur himself, and fashions it with twelve seats, with one place left empty to mark the betrayal of Judas. This seat – known to French writers as the 'siege perilous' or 'perilous seat' – must remain empty until the coming of the knight who will finally discover the Holy Grail. In other Vulgate Cycle tales the Round Table is a wedding gift to Arthur from Guinevere's father, King Leodagan of Carmelide. All these works would have been immensely popular when Winchester's Round Table was constructed – and, moreover, they were considered works of courtly literature that were intended to be read or performed in front of a royal or baronial court, to a secular audience of nobles and, increasingly, a burgeoning merchant class whose members were beginning to acquire the tastes of their noble counterparts. The Round Table in Winchester Castle might well have been built for such an event, either creating or strengthening a medieval tradition that identified the city as Camelot.

Caerleon and Caerwent

Geoffrey of Monmouth never mentioned Camelot in his *Historia*. Nonetheless he provided a description of the location and ambience of Arthur's principal court, and though he only named it as the 'City of the Legion', it is clear that the town Geoffrey was describing was Caerleon, situated only 20 miles southwest of his home town of Monmouth, across the border in Wales. Caerleon lies immediately to the north of the down-at-heel industrial town of Newport, and looking at it on a map it would be tempting to think that it was part of its northern spread. But this is not the case; Caerleon is a country town in its own right, with an appealingly crooked high street that runs down to an equally appealing reach of the River Usk, wide and confident here (and still tidal) as it describes a broad loop through a low range of hills. Caerleon's centre occupies the floor of the deep valley, with a thickly wooded ridge separating the town from Newport, giving it a definite sense of separateness from the sprawl of the South Wales coast and the constant thrum of the M4 motorway. Visitors would be hard pressed to believe that less than 3 miles away from Caerleon (as the crow flies) is the site of the former Llanwern steelworks, once an industrial powerhouse but largely derelict since its closure in 2001 (though Tata Steel continues some operations there).

Just off Caerleon's High Street are the remains of some Roman baths. The complex boasts curving ducts for hot air and water, scraps of mosaics, and pillared foundations – all housed in a pavilion and with child-friendly displays to keep all the clipboard-wielding schoolkids happy. Around 200 yards away, surrounded by nondescript open ground beside the Usk, is a grassed-over Roman amphitheatre dating from around AD 90, with the stone base of the seating and some of the original paving still intact (this is, in fact, the most thoroughly excavated amphitheatre in Britain). Across the road from the amphitheatre the excavated outlines of four rows of barracks blocks are picked out in a field. The setting is mundane – suburban semis fringe the field on three sides – but the barracks must have been a grim place in Roman times. The most discernible building on the site is a latrine block,

Above and overleaf: The Roman amphitheatre at Caerleon - its circular shape could provide an origin for the legend of the Round Table and Camelot. (*Andrew Beattie*)

The Roman amphitheatre at Caerleon. (*Andrew Beattie*)

its deep drain still intact. The site is a noisy place to visit mid-afternoon in term time, when the adjacent comprehensive school empties and its pupils head for the school buses, parked on the roadside that divides the barracks from the amphitheatre. The two sites, along with the baths, are the visible remnants of a Roman fortress known as Isca Augusta (or Isca Silurum), which during the later Roman era served as one of only three legionary fortresses on the island of Britain (the other two were at Chester and York). It is assumed that the remains of other buildings lie under the suburban spread of Caerleon; in 2011 parts of a Roman harbour were discovered on the banks of the Usk, which is wide enough here to support barge traffic. The fortress was constructed in around AD 74, when the Romans had finally quelled and subdued the Silures tribe, who had resisted their advances into South Wales for decades. The ramparts were originally of earth and timber, but an inscription of Trajan gives a date of AD 99/100 for their replacement with a stone revetment backed by a clay bank and fronted by a single ditch. The interior of the camp was fitted out with the usual array of military buildings; a headquarters building, legate's residence, tribunes' houses, a

The latrine block is one of the best preserved parts of the Roman barracks at Caerleon. (*Andrew Beattie*)

hospital, workshops and granaries were present alongside the baths and the barrack blocks and the amphitheatre. The camp was occupied until at least 380 and might have still been garrisoned when the Romans pulled out of Britain some three decades later. When the site was abandoned, the ancient baths were used as a cattle pen and the stone was gradually pilfered.

It is possible that Geoffrey of Monmouth took the name 'City of the Legion' from Nennius, who gave this name to one of Arthur's battles that he described in his *Historia Brittonum* (AD 830). It is debateable whether Nennius's 'City of the Legion' was actually Caerleon. However, Geoffrey's definitely is. 'When the feast of Whitsuntide began to draw near,' Geoffrey recounts,

> Arthur ... made up his mind to hold a plenary court at that season and place the crown of the kingdom on his head. He decided too, to summon to this feast the leaders who owed him homage, so that he could celebrate Whitsun with greater reverence and renew the closest pacts of peace with his chieftains. He explained to the members of his

107

court what he was proposing to do and accepted their advice that he should carry out his plan in the City of the Legions. Situated as it is in Morgannwg [Glamorgan], on the River Usk, not far from the Severn Sea, in a most pleasant position, and being richer in material wealth than other townships, this city was eminently suitable for such a ceremony. The river which I have named flowed by it on one side, and up this the kings and princes who were to come from across the sea could be carried in a fleet of ships. On the other side, which was flanked by meadows and wooded groves, they had adorned the city with royal palaces, and by the gold-painted gables of its roofs it was a match for Rome.

While many scholars and Arthur enthusiasts argue about the location or even the existence of Camelot, few could disagree that Geoffrey's description of the court held at Caerleon was inspirational for a later generation of writers. When Chrétien de Troyes wrote about Camelot it is almost inconceivable that the inspiration for this creation was not the Caerleon described by Geoffrey. Thomas Malory makes many references to Caerleon, including an indication that this was where Arthur was crowned, and though he placed Camelot firmly in Winchester, his champion William Caxton states in his preface to *Morte d'Arthur* that he considers Camelot to be in Wales and gives a description that sounds very much like Caerleon, 'the great stones and the marvellous works of iron lying underground, and the royal vaults which many now living have seen.' The writer T.H. White, who derived considerable inspiration from Malory, set the wedding of King Pellinore that takes place in the second volume of *The Once and Future King* in the town (naming it Carlion), writing that, 'the metropolitan glories … were enough to take [one's] breath away' and describing the,

> walled town … that was surrounded by a battlement which seemed to go on for ever and ever. The wall had towers every two hundred yards, and four great gates as well. When you were approaching the town from across the plain, you could see the castle keeps and church spires springing out of the wall in a clump – like flowers growing in a pot.

The associations of Caerleon with King Arthur have also provided inspiration for poets. One was Thomas Churchyard, who was born the son of a farmer near Shrewsbury in around 1520, and served as a soldier in Scotland, Ireland, the Low Countries and France before becoming a writer. His 1587 work *The Worthiness of Wales* was dedicated to Queen Elizabeth I (in whose court he unsuccessfully tried to seek a position) and provides a description of that country in verse. After describing Monmouth, Raglan, Chepstow and Usk, Churchyard turns his attention to the 'famous town' of Caerleon: 'Thou hast been great, though now of little worth,' he says. 'Thy noble bounds hath reached beyond them all; / In thee hath been King Arthur's golden hall. / In thee the wise and worthies did repose, / And through thy town the water ebbs and flows.' Churchyard portrays the town as the historic seat of many kings, before stating that 'King Arthur sure was crowned there, / It was his royal seat, / And in this town did sceptre bear, / With pomp and honour great. / An Archbishop, that Dubric hight / Did crown this King in deed.' Churchyard also writes that 'In Arthur's time a table round / Was there whereat he sate' – a reference to the circular Roman amphitheatre being traditionally known as King Arthur's Round Table.

It was to Caerleon that Tennyson repaired when he was writing his verse cycle *Idylls of the King* in 1856. He lodged in the Hanbury Arms, a riverside inn around 300 metres from both the amphitheatre and the Roman baths, where he could seek inspiration by looking out over the River Usk, and going for long walks through the surrounding countryside. Most of the Hanbury Arms dates from around 1565 when it was built as a residence for the prominent Morgan family. Little of the structure has changed over the years – although its usage has. At one time the local magistrates heard cases here, in a panelled room, and miscreants would be locked in the circular defensive tower which is incongruously attached to the pub and is thought to date from the thirteenth century (when plundered Roman stones were used to build it). Immediately below the pub is the ancient quay from where small ships once set out for places such as Bristol and ports along the coast of Southwest England and South Wales; there was even a tramway linking the quay with Cwmbran, to bring in metal ore for export. But Tennyson's poetic musings do not seem to have been disturbed by any shouts from the quayside or the clang of ships unloading. On 16 September 1856

Left: Alfred, Lord Tennyson, photographed by Lewis Carroll. (*Source, Wikimedia Commons*)

Below: The Hanbury Arms, beside the River Usk in Caerleon, where Tennyson wrote his verse epic *Idylls of the King*. (*Andrew Beattie*)

he wrote to his wife Emily that 'The Usk murmurs by the windows and I sit like King Arthur at Caerleon. I came here last night from Newport. This is a most quiet village of about 1,500 inhabitants with a little museum of Roman tombstones and other things.' On the following day Tennyson wrote again to his sister claiming that he was trying to remain incognito, worried that Mr Jones, the local vicar, and 'Mr Lee, a landed proprietor who lives in a large house near the amphitheatre', would recognise him. (The 'large house' was the Priory, and 'Mr Lee' was John Edward Lee, an antiquary and geologist and author of books on Roman Caerleon, who in 1850 founded Caerleon's Roman Museum, which remains an attraction in the town today.) 'I suppose they have found me out, though they have never alluded to my status,' Tennyson concludes.

His great poem mentions Caerleon a number of times. On one occasion Arthur 'held court at old Caerleon upon Usk. / There on a day, he sitting high in hall, / Before him came a forester of Dean, / Wet from the woods, with notice of a hart / Taller than all his fellows, milky-white, / First seen that day.' Arthur promptly gives, order to let blow / His horns for hunting on the morrow morn.' On another occasion Arthur

> 'sat / In hall at old Caerleon, the high doors / Were softly sundered, and through these a youth, / Pelleas, and the sweet smell of the fields / Past, and the sunshine came along with him.

Pelleas demands that Arthur makes him a knight, 'because I know, Sir King, / All that belongs to knighthood,' before relating how he has won the love of his lady, Ettarre.

Today the Hanbury Arms – where these lines might well have been written – is a fine and very spacious historic country pub, with a pleasant terrace (the former quayside) and a view downriver to the elegant nineteenth-century road bridge that is a successor to the Roman and medieval timber bridges that once stood adjacent to the inn. Tennyson is remembered by a circular blue plaque on the outside of the building that proclaims that this was where he 'began writing' his famous work, and another plaque beside a bay window in the main lounge installed by Monmouthshire Local History Society in 1956 that 'commemorates the visit by Alfred, Lord Tennyson to this historic inn during September 1856'.

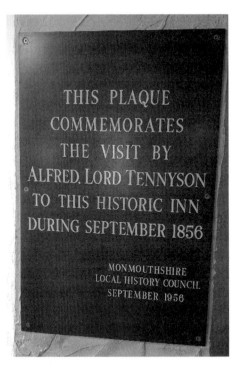

Left: A plaque in the Hanbury Arms, beside the River Usk in Caerleon, where Tennyson wrote his verse epic *Idylls of the King*. (*Courtesy Hanbury Arms*)

Below: A plaque on the exterior wall of the Hanbury Arms. (*Andrew Beattie*)

Lodge Hill and Caerwent

Caerleon's history did not begin and end with the Romans. A large hill-fort was constructed on what is now the Northwest fringes of Caerleon around four centuries before their arrival – the stronghold, perhaps, of the legendary Beli, King of Britain. When the Romans left Britain many of the ancient hill-forts such as this one on Lodge Hill were reoccupied – and some maintain that King Arthur held court not on the old Roman site (which would have been too large to defend) but on Lodge Hill. In the Summer of 2000 the University of Wales, Newport (which at the time maintained a campus at Caerleon), conducted excavations on the site that uncovered post-holes, the stone surfaces of buildings and evidence of industrial activity in the form of slag from iron working; among the artefacts unearthed were mid- and late Iron Age pottery and an iron brooch from around 300 BC. Other findings, including shards of pottery, indicate that the hill-fort was reused and possibly reoccupied in the late Roman period. It is possible that the inner rampart may have been rebuilt during this time or during the immediate post-Roman period – the time of Arthur. Unfortunately there is nothing to draw visitors to this site, which is accessed via a road called Lodge Hill, a residential street that leads up from the centre of Caerleon through a prosperous-looking estate of modern houses. On the site of the camp itself some ramparts and ditches are discernible, but all are smothered in thick woodland and undergrowth and really this place (exceptionally muddy after rain) is best left to dog walkers and weekend ramblers rather than those with an interest in King Arthur.

Five miles east of Caerleon is a much smaller settlement named Caerwent. This is a village rather than a town, and is located just a couple of miles from Chepstow and the English border. At the time of the Roman invasion this site, like Lodge Hill, was occupied by the Silures tribe, who fought back vigorously against the occupiers, as the large number of Roman fortresses in the area (more than in any other part of Britain) suggests. There is some dispute as to whether the Silures were actually defeated by the Romans, or persuaded to work with them. Certainly Caerwent, known in those days as Venta Silurum, soon became the administrative centre and capital of the Silures, who cooperated with the Romans, helping them maintain and supply their large garrisons in the area. Today Caerwent, an otherwise unremarkable place, is home to an extraordinary feature of international importance – namely, its Roman

Left: Caerwent boasts some of the most substantial Roman walls in Europe. Some have suggested that this is the true site of Arthur's Camelot. (*Andrew Beattie*)

Below: Outlines and remains of Roman buildings at Caerwent. (*Andrew Beattie*)

Above and below: Outlines and remains of Roman buildings at Caerwent. (*Andrew Beattie*)

walls, which surround the village and are counted as some of the most impressive of their type in northern Europe; scattered across the village are other Roman remains, including a spacious forum. The remains poke up in green spaces between houses, though most are little more than outlines and foundations, with very little extending above waist height. The ensemble is surprising – not many English villages have their own temple ruins – and in places the Roman walls are truly impressive, standing several metres tall and sporting bastions and defensive towers. Caerwent is rarely associated with King Arthur, but one hypothesis suggests that Malory had actually intended to locate Camelot at Caerwent but somehow Venta Silurum became confused with Venta Belgarum, the Roman name for Winchester. But he left tentative clues suggesting that he might have meant Caerwent rather than Winchester. In *Le Morte d'Arthur* Malory states that twelve of Arthur's defeated enemies 'were buried in the Church of St Stephen's in Camelot', and that Arthur 'the King was wedded at Camelot unto Dame Guenever in the Church of St Stephen's, with great solemnity'. Caerwent has a church dedicated to St Stephen located at the settlement's heart, within the old Roman walls, much-visited because of the Roman tombstones on display inside; although Winchester has two churches dedicated to the same saint, neither is in the city centre – so is Winchester an interloper, and this village in Southeast Wales, with its Roman walls and tombstones and Church of St Stephen, the real site of Camelot?

Cadbury Castle

Credible though their claims to be the 'genuine' Camelot may be, Caerwent and Caerleon are given a considerable run for their money by an ancient hill-fort located deep in the county of Somerset. In fact, in many ways Cadbury Castle, situated 5 miles northeast of Yeovil and easily accessible from the main A303 road that links London and Exeter, holds much more appeal as a destination for visitors, free as it is of the modern encumbrances of houses, shops, and roads that despoil the two Welsh contenders. But the first thing to understand about this site is that there is no castle here, and nor has there ever been; instead, the 'castle' consists of a limestone mound located on the southern edge of the Somerset Levels, whose grassy, undulating and spacious summit, some 153 metres above sea level, was once home to one of the largest hill-forts in Britain. Today all there is to be seen here of historic interest are terraced earthwork that take the form of substantial banks and ditches. Yet Cadbury Castle has a history of occupation stretching from the Neolithic era to the Middle Ages – and some historians, most famously Geoffrey Ashe, have championed this place as the site of King Arthur's Camelot, though as usual any 'evidence' linking this site with King Arthur is nothing more than tangential.

Hill-forts such as Cadbury Castle developed in the late Bronze and early Iron Ages, around the start of the first millennium BC. The reason for their emergence in prehistoric Britain and their exact purpose has been a subject of some considerable debate. It has been argued that they could have been military sites constructed in response to invasion from continental Europe; or that they were fortifications built by those invaders; or that they were a political response to simmering social tensions fomented by an increasing population and the consequent pressure on agriculture and trade – particularly in iron and copper, which were mined in different locations on the island of Britain though had to be brought to the same place for smelting. Whatever the reason for the foundation of the Iron Age hill-fort at South

Above and overleaf: Ramparts and ditches of Cadbury Castle - one of the contenders for Camelot. (*Andrew Beattie*)

Cadbury, it was not the first settlement that occupied this commanding outpost. Pits and post holes hint at the existence here of a small agricultural settlement during the Neolithic era, and bones recovered from the site have been radiocarbon dated to around 3400 BC. Finds from the Bronze Age include the earliest shield unearthed during an archaeological excavation in northwest Europe; the artefact has subsequently been dated to around 1200 BC and can be seen in the Museum of Somerset in Taunton. During the Iron Age the settlement comprised a stone enclosure and ramparts that surrounded roundhouses and temples, all of which was refortified several times until the Romans occupied the site in the late first century. Excavations of the southwest gate in 1968 and 1969 revealed evidence for one or more severe violent episodes from the early Roman period, which might have been the result of vigorous local resistance to the second Augusta Legion under the command of Vespasian. There was significant activity at the site during the late third and fourth centuries, which may have included the construction of a Romano-British temple, and for a century or so after the Romans left, the fort was resettled yet again, only to be abandoned in around 580. Between 1010 and 1020, when Britain was under severe threat

118

of Viking invasion, a mint was set up here, briefly taking over the role of the mint at Ilchester, some 5 miles away, an important town in those days, though nowadays little more than a village. Some small-scale refortification of the site may also have been carried out during the later Middle Ages.

The village of Queen Camel near Cadbury Castle. Its name may be related to Arthur's legendary fort of Camelot. (*Andrew Beattie*)

The fort's name probably derives from the River Cam, whose course lies around a mile north of Cadbury Castle and which also gives its name to the villages of West Camel and Queen Camel, the latter worth a visit for its beautifully preserved (and pedestrianised) gently curving street of thatched cottages that leads to the village church. Another possible derivation is that the name Cadbury comes from 'Cado's fort' – Cado being a sixth-century ruler of Dumnonia, the Dark Age kingdom whose easternmost defensive outpost this might have been.

The first author to identify Cadbury Castle as Camelot was John Leland, Henry VIII's topographer and antiquary, who came this way in 1542 when compiling a survey of the monuments of Southwest England. 'At the very south end of the church of South Cadbury stands Camallate,' he wrote, 'sometime a famous town or castle, upon a very tor or hill, wonderfully strengthened by nature, to the which be two enterings up by a very steep way.' Leland goes on to write of the Roman-era gold and coins found in the area and that the 'people can tell nothing there but that they have heard say that Arthur much resorted to Camalat … diverse villages there about bere the name Camalat by an addition, as Queen-Camallat, and others.' It is likely that Leland was recording a local tradition that this distinctive natural mount had indeed been the site of King Arthur's Camelot. His comments are echoed by a later antiquarian, William Camden, whose survey *Britannia* was published in 1586. In the section on Somerset Camden describes 'Camalet' as,

> a steepe hill and hard to get up; on the top whereof are to bee seene expresse tokens of a decayed Castle with triple rampires of earth cast up, enclosing within it many acres of ground, and there appeare about the hill five or six ditches, so steepe that a man shall sooner slide downe than goe downe. The Inhabitants name it King Arthur's Palace … As for Cadburie, a little towne next unto it, we may ghesse verie probably to have been that Cathbregion where King Arthur (as Ninnius writeth) defeated the English-Saxons in a memorable battell.

The site has been subject to a number of archaeological excavations. The first person to investigate the site, during the explosion of interest in archaeology during the Victorian era, was a local clergyman, Revd James Bennett, who was the rector of South Cadbury, the village that clings to the north-eastern skirts of the castle mound. Bennett cut a section through the top rampart and concluded that it had been built up in layers over a long period of time, but his successor, Harold St George Gray, went one stage further during his investigations in 1913, when he unearthed artefacts from the late Iron Age. In the 1950s part of the enclosure was ploughed, and a local archaeologist, Mary Harfield, examined flints and potsherds which lay exposed in the upturned soil. Among these, Dr Ralegh Radford, the famed archaeologist of Tintagel, recognised pottery of a type he had found there; he concluded that its provenance and quality suggested that whoever had lived at Cadbury Castle possessed sufficient wealth and standing to import luxury goods from continental Europe. Radford's findings led to the formation of the Camelot Research Committee, which carried out large-scale excavations from 1966 to 1970 under the direction of Professor Leslie Alcock (1925–2006), one of the most celebrated archaeologists of his time, whose name became indelibly associated in the public's imagination with the search for King Arthur's Camelot. Alcock was a colourful character and a skilful self-publicist who managed to excite much attention from the press over his work (he later became a familiar figure on television). His sense of humour also came out during the excavations – he had a good understanding of what visitors to the site wanted to see, so he had a plastic skeleton excavated from the same spot every afternoon, with a bucket beside the trench to take donations for the diggers' 'welfare fund' (much of which ended up in the coffers of the local pub).

Alcock's investigations revealed that a village had flourished on the plateau for hundreds of years before the Romans stormed the castle and evicted the survivors, resettling them at the foot of the hill. During most of the Roman period the enclosure was empty, although it is thought that a pagan temple might have been built in the fourth century AD. Alcock's most exciting discovery was that the fort had been refortified in the late fifth or early sixth century, and remained occupied until sometime after 580 – the era of King Arthur. The main evidence for this reoccupation came in the form of foundations of a timber hall, 63 ft by 34 ft, its walls defined by post-holes cut in the bedrock, possibly modelled on the villa complexes of later Roman Britain; at the south-west entry were the remains of a gatehouse consisting of a square wooden tower, approached by a cobbled road 10 ft wide, which would have passed through two sets of double doors on either side of the gatehouse. This complex was discovered on the high part of the plateau that had been known as 'Arthur's Place' since the sixteenth century. Most important of all was the discovery that the surrounding rampart had been massively rebuilt in Arthurian times, providing a defended site double the size of any other known fort of the period. Although there was nothing with Arthur's name on it, what Alcock and his team found suggested that a leader with considerable resources at his command had taken possession of the vacant hill-fort and refortified it on a colossal scale. At the centre of the fort that leader built at least one substantial building and probably several smaller ones, enough to house not only his family, but also an army of retainers, servants and horses. At the time he was excavating Cadbury, Alcock was inclined to believe that Arthur was a historical figure, a view reflected in his 1971 book *Arthur's Britain*. In later life, though, Alcock distanced himself from the book, having become convinced that in fact there was no good evidence that Arthur ever existed. 'There are no historically acceptable accounts, so it's pretty futile to try and identify where Camelot may or may not have been,' he admitted in 1999. However, he continued to maintain that, if Arthur had lived anywhere, Cadbury Castle was the most likely site, as it defended the approach to Devon and Cornwall from the rest of Southern England.

Another historian who also believed that Cadbury Castle was Camelot was Geoffrey Ashe, who was a major proponent of the theory that the historical King Arthur was Riothamus, a Romano-British leader of the fifth century; in the 1960s he was co-founder of the Camelot Research Committee which commissioned Alcock's archaeological investigations at the site. 'I would say there must have been a tradition about the hill and its powerful overlord, handed down from the Dark Ages,' Ashe declared, adding that, 'In the film of the musical *Camelot*, you have a brief glimpse of a map of Britain, and Camelot is in Somerset. It's there because I told Warner Brothers to put it there. That is my one contribution to Hollywood.'

Since Alcock's excavations concluded, the public interest in South Cadbury has waned, though the place still exerts a draw; easily accessible by foot (in under ten minutes) along a steep track that leads up through trees from the southern end of South Cadbury village, the site covers a large area of uneven ground, with its formidable defensive banks and ditches (worn bare by walkers at their summits) more clearly defined than those of other Iron Age hill-forts – the result perhaps of comparatively recent refortification. This is a large site too, a circumnavigation of the outer walls takes a good quarter of an hour. While the slopes of the fort are covered in a tangle of thick woodland, the upper part consists of a lumpy plateau of bare grass, with a cairn at its highest point and a plaque ('Cadbury Castle AD 2000') with arrows pointing out the distance and direction to other Arthurian sites, including Tintagel. The views are spectacular for such a short walk; in one direction the forests and farms reach as far as the outskirts of the market town of Yeovil, while in the other the distinctive point of St Michael's church on the summit of Glastonbury Tor is clearly discernible across a level, English landscape of fields, woodland and villages. The only thing that detracts from the rural appeal is the grind of traffic along the A303; it threads its way past the camp on one of its many dual carriageway sections, dividing the village of North Cadbury from South Cadbury – which is barely a mile from a signposted junction on the road. The Camelot Pub overlooks the crossroads at the centre of the village; its walls are covered in yellowing newspaper cuttings and other memorabilia from Alcock's archaeological excavations. On the path down from the fort, a cheeky sign beside the

Direction indicator at the centre of Cadbury Castle, pointing the way to a number of other Arthurian sites. (*Andrew Beattie*)

123

The Camelot pub in South Cadbury village, whose walls are covered in newspaper cuttings relating to the excavation works at Cadbury Castle nearby. (*Andrew Beattie*)

track asks walkers if they are 'still looking for the castle' (a reference to the fort's somewhat misleading name; there has never been a castle here) and suggests that 'to clear the mists of legends, come to the Camelot!' The pub, village and 'castle' stand at the nexus of a small outpost of geographical Arthuriana; the clutch of ten village churches around South Cadbury have styled themselves the 'Camelot Parishes' and one of the churches, at North Cheriton, even advertises 'Camelot Matins' on selected Sunday mornings, while children in the area can get involved in the 'young Camelot' group. Not surprisingly, Arthurian legends abound; one tells that Arthur and his knights are sleeping in one of the caves beneath Cadbury Castle, waiting for a time when the people of Britain need them again. The entrance to their cave is an iron gate that's guarded by a giant; he opens the gate once every seven years on Midsummer's day, letting the men ride the land for one night only each year. A number of authors, including Marion Zimmer Bradley (in her *Mists of Avalon* series) and Mary Stewart (in her Arthurian sagas later collected as *The Merlin Trilogy*), were also inspired enough by Alcock's investigations to place their Camelots in South Cadbury.

The Camel valley, Colchester and other Camelot Contenders

Of the other contenders to be the 'original' Camelot, Cornwall's Camel valley lays the most convincing claim – even if the basis for this is simply down to it being in Cornwall (the site of most Arthurian legends) and, of course, bearing an almost identical name to Arthur's mystical fortress. Yet the major town on the upper Camel, Camelford, makes nothing of its Arthurian heritage. (Camelford and the Camel valley are discussed in the next chapter as they also lay claim to being the site of Arthur's last battle, at Camlann.) Another possible contender is Colchester, which was named Camulodunum by the Romans after Camulus, a Celtic god, and was championed by the historian John Morris as Camelot in his influential book *The Age of Arthur*. Morris reasoned that as the descendants of Romanised Britons looked back to a golden age of peace and prosperity under Roman rule, the name 'Camelot' may have referred to the capital of Britannia in Roman times. However, Colchester was located well within the territory that was conquered early in the fifth century by the Saxons, so making it unlikely to have been the location for Camelot. Even the Colchester Museum argues strongly against any links to King Arthur, maintaining that 'It would be impossible and inconceivable to link him to the Colchester area, or to Essex more generally,' and pointing out that the connection between the name Camulodunum and Colchester was unknown until the eighteenth century.

The former Roman fort of Cambodunum near Huddersfield seems a more likely claimant, though once again the only real 'evidence' to suggest this comes from its name and from its strategic location close to the southern borders of the former kingdom of Hen Ogledd, which occupied modern-day northern England and southern Scotland. Also known as Slack Roman Fort, this fortification guarded the Pennine section of the Roman road from Deva Victrix (Chester) to Eboracum (York). Archaeological digs indicate the fort was constructed in the time of Agricola, in AD 79, to defend the road, and that it was a complex of buildings of turf and wood. Excavations in the nineteenth century uncovered the remains of a palatial residence, along with items of pottery and jewellery; later digs, carried out in the 1910s and between 1958 and 1963, uncovered the fort's ramparts and the foundations of its gateways and corner towers. There is nothing to see of it now; the former fort lies hidden beneath the car park of a golf club, while the M62 motorway roars nearby (and at this point is built on top of the old Roman road). In December 2016, a retired professor from Bangor University, Peter Field, claimed he had 'probably found Camelot' here, but admitted to the *Huddersfield Examiner*,

> There is no certainty. The evidence is not thick enough on the ground for anybody to be certain of anything. You have to go on what you know. It does not mean Arthur was born there or buried there but it means the people who told the stories saw that it was his place.

Field's discovery certainly thrilled writer Simon Keegan, author of the book *Pennine Dragon*, who earlier in the same year had identified King Arthur with a northern British king named Arthwys ap Mar and had also located Camelot at Slack. However the theory does not seem to have gained currency among either academics or the dedicated community of amateur Arthurians.

Chapter Three

The End of Arthur

Glastonbury, the Camel Valley and Dozmary Pool

Camlann and Avalon

Geoffrey of Monmouth describes the end of Arthur in appropriately epic and bloodthirsty terms. Arthur is slain by his mortal enemy Mordred following a final, apocalyptic battle fought at Camlann, and Geoffrey provides an elaborately-wrought backstory to these events involving all the great elements of epic storytelling – passionate love, greedy treachery and deadly betrayal. Up until this last part of the story, Arthur's life has been one of triumph. He has married Guenhuuara, the daughter of a Cornish nobleman (whom Thomas Malory later renames Guinevere), defeated the Picts and the Scots and created an empire that encompassed Ireland, Iceland, Orkney, Norway and Denmark. Now Arthur has even grander military ambitions to pursue, and he crosses the Channel to Gaul to engage the Romans. But as he prepares to march on Rome he hears that his nephew Modredus (Thomas Malory's Mordred) – whom he had left in charge of Britain – has betrayed him by marrying Guenhuuara and seizing the throne. Seething at Mordred's duplicity, Arthur returns to Britain to hunt down his treacherous nephew.

From the outset Arthur's campaign is vicious, bloody and personal. But Mordred gains the upper hand, pursuing Arthur 'into [Cornwall] as far as the river Cambula', where he,

> placed his troops in order, resolving either to conquer or to
> die, rather than continue his flight any longer ... Arthur, on
> the other side, also marshalled his army, which he divided

into nine square companies, with a right and left wing; and having appointed to each of them their commanders, exhorted them to make a total rout of those robbers and perjured villains, who, being brought over into the island from foreign countries at the instance of the arch-traitor, were attempting to rob them of all their honours.

Battle then erupts,

> [in] great fury; wherein it would be both grievous and tedious to relate the slaughter, the cruel havoc, and the excess of fury that was to be seen on both sides. In this manner they spent a good part of the day, till Arthur at last made a push with his company, consisting of six thousand six hundred and sixty-six men, against that in which he knew Modredus was; and having opened a way with their swords, they pierced quite through it, and made a grievous slaughter. For in this assault fell the wicked traitor himself, and many thousands with him.

But even as he celebrates Mordred's death, Arthur finds himself to be mortally wounded. So he gives up the crown of Britain to his kinsman Constantine, the son of Cador, Duke of Cornwall, and is 'carried thence to the isle of Avalon to be cured of his wounds.'

This was not the first time that this last great battle of Arthur's had appeared in literature. The *Annales Cambriae*, written around two centuries before Geoffrey's *Historia*, identifies 'the battle of Camlann' as the occasion on which both Arthur and Mordred die, though the anonymous compiler of this work does not say who won the battle or whether Arthur and Mordred were enemies. Camlann is also identified in the Welsh Triads as the third and bloodiest of the 'three futile battles' that Arthur fought. It appears that Geoffrey of Monmouth took these slivers of material and from them wove his fantastical tale of Arthur's final days and hours. And for chroniclers who came after Geoffrey this was too good a fantasy to ignore. Miastre Wace, who translated Geoffrey's work into Norman French, also provides a vividly bloody portrait of the slaughter at Camlann. 'Many people were slain on either side,' he wrote, 'so that the field was strewn with the dead, and was crimson with the blood of dying men. There perished the brave and comely youth Arthur had gathered from so many lands. Arthur himself was wounded and wondrously much. Fifteen dreadful wounds he had.' After bequeathing his kingdom to Constantine, Arthur announces that he will 'fare to Avalon ... but afterwards I will come again to my kingdom, and dwell with the Britons with much joy'. Then 'there came a boat borne on the waves, and two women therein wondrously arrayed, and they took Arthur and bore him quickly, and softly laid him down, and fared forth away.' Malory, in turn, provides yet another version of these events, claiming that the battle is sparked off when a knight draws his sword against an adder that slithers by – which immediately prompts the other knights to draw their swords, too. 'Never was there seen a more doleful battle,' he wrote. 'They fought all day long, and never stinted until the noble knights were laid to the cold earth; and ever they fought still till it was near night, and by that time was there a hundred thousand laid dead upon the down.' At the battle's end, as the dead lie all around them, Arthur and Mordred engage in one final bout of violence; Arthur kills Mordred and is led away to a small chapel as robbers descend to steal from the dead knights that scatter the battlefield. On the shores of a lake, Arthur commands Sir Bedevere to throw his sword Excalibur into the water, before he is taken off by barge to the Vale of Avalon.

Avalon (Geoffrey has it as Avallon) is Geoffrey of Monmouth's invention. In *Vita Merlini* (*The Life of Merlin*), which was later incorporated into his *Historia*, he identifies Avalon as 'the island of apples, which men called "the fortunate isle"' – fortunate in that an endless supply of grapes, grain and apples grow naturally there without the need for any cultivation. But while he may be the first to name Avalon, the place has a clear pedigree – for Geoffrey's Avalon is none other than the 'Elysian Fields' that feature in early Greek literature. These islands are a paradise on earth to which heroes retire at the end of their active careers. They were a popular subject for Roman writers, such as the geographer Pomponius Mela, who described the islands as being located off Brittany and populated by nine priestesses who performed acts of healing to the wounded warriors who finished up there. As to the name for these British Elysian Fields, Geoffrey seems to have derived 'Avalon' from 'aball', a word in Old Welsh meaning 'fruit' or 'apple tree' that alludes to the bounteousness of the island – and to the apple tree in the Garden of Eden, that other worldly paradise that, like Avalon, was preparatory to Heaven. Geoffrey was the first writer to link King Arthur with such an island (he also claimed Excalibur was forged there) but his successors were happy to follow suit. Maistre Wace noted that Avalon was the place where Arthur went 'for treatment of his wounds. He is still there, awaited by the Britons, as they say and believe, and will return and may live again,' while the English poet Layamon has the injured Arthur tell his assembled men that once he is on the island he will go to 'Argante the queen, fairest of fairy women, and she shall make well my wounds.'

Geoffrey clearly identifies Camlann as having been fought on the banks of the River Camel in Cornwall; a site at the appropriately named hamlet of Slaughterbridge, close to the town of Camelford, has been suggested as a possible location – though if Geoffrey's version is assumed to be a fiction, other sites also emerge as contenders, including a number outside Cornwall. As to Avalon and the pool that was the home of Excalibur and the Lady of the Lake – well, any number of locations in Cornwall, Somerset and Wales make the claim to be the prototype for this imaginative flight of fancy. (They include a town in Burgundy named Avalon, situated on the banks of the River Yonne – though like Geoffrey's Avalon, this place might also simply derive its name from the Celtic word for 'apple'.) But it is the Somerset town of Glastonbury, above all, that claims the crown as the place where Arthur's death is fully commemorated. For here there are ancient ties to the legend of the Holy Grail, and a domed hill that was once an island surrounded by water, making it the perfect prototype for Avalon; even more, a hoax perpetrated by some twelfth-century monks wanting to raise money to rebuild their fire-damaged abbey has cemented Glastonbury's enduring place in Arthurian legend, seemingly for eternity.

Camelford and Slaughterbridge: King Arthur's Final Battle

Just as history has bequeathed the story of Arthur's conception and birth to Cornwall, so too does this ancient land at the southwest tip of Britain lay claim to be the place where Arthur met his end. Geoffrey of Monmouth named Tintagel as the place Arthur was conceived and, searching for a place where Arthur fought his last battle, named the Camel valley, only a short distance inland from the stormy north coast, as the site. Later writers were happy to follow suit. Thus these writers invested their narratives with a geographical authenticity that went some way to compensating for

130

their tales' lack of authenticity of the historical kind. And so it is on the banks of the River Camel that the quest begins for the place where Arthur fought his final battle.

The Camel is one of the longest rivers in Cornwall. Rising on the northern slopes of Bodmin Moor, it describes a broad loop as it flows southwest towards Bodmin and then – without actually passing through the ancient market town – switches course, turning west and then north towards the sea. The largest settlement the Camel passes through is Wadebridge, a workaday town situated at the place where the river widens into its beautiful estuary. Beyond Wadebridge 'holiday' Cornwall begins; the fishing towns of Padstow and Rock, swarming with tourists in the summer, cling to the shores of the Camel estuary where it meets the Atlantic. It is, of course, the river's exotic and unusual name that makes it a prime contender for the location of both Camlann, Arthur's final battle, and Camelot, Arthur's legendary court. Geoffrey of Monmouth located the latter in Wales but placed the site of Camlann in Cornwall, without saying precisely where. His successor and translator Maistre Wace went one stage further, claiming that Arthur's final battle was waged on the banks of the River Camel 'over against the entrance to Cornwall', alluding to the fact that Devon begins some 15 miles east of the Camel's source. The poet Layamon narrows the location of Camlann down even further, naming the town of Camelford, on the River Camel, as the actual site of the battlefield; when the fighting here was over, he writes, 'the stream hard-by was flooded with blood unmeasured.'

Layamon was active during the reign of King John – that is, between 1199 and 1216. So the legends linking Camelford with King Arthur go back at least 800 years. They were certainly well entrenched in the area by the 1530s when the topographer John Leland recorded in his survey of Cornwall that 'By this Ryver Arture fought his last Field, yn token wherof the People fynd there yn plowing bones and harneys [people find when ploughing bones and harnesses].' By this time the exact site of the battle had now been narrowed down to a small hamlet named Slaughterbridge, a mile upstream from the town of Camelford; it was in fields flanking the Camel immediately north of Slaughterbridge that all the finds that Leland alludes to had been made – and in 1602 the Cornish antiquary Richard Carew also commented on them. 'Upon the river of Camel, neere to Camelford, was that last dismal battel strooken betweene the noble king Arthur and his treacherous nephew Mordred,' he wrote, 'wherein the one took his death, and the other his death's wound.' An account that appeared in the *Royal Cornwall Gazette* on 1 February 1850 confirmed John Leland's descriptions of the 'bones and harneys' (horses' harnesses) being unearthed from the fields on which the great battle had been fought.

> While some labourers were employed a few weeks since in excavating for the foundations of a house at Slaughter Bridge, near Camelford, they dug up some implements of ancient war, consisting of a battle axe, a spear, and a spur, supposed to have lain buried there since the days of king Arthur ... The persons who found the articles named gave them away, setting but little value on them ... the spur is now in the possession of Mr Creeper of the White Hart Inn.

Polsue's *Complete Parochial History of the County of Cornwall* of 1867 includes a similar account of 'several spear heads of iron' being discovered, 'and at a short distance from the same place the blade of a small scimitar-shaped sword in good condition was discovered two or three feet under the surface.'

Various suggestions have been put forward as to why the area around Slaughterbridge has yielded so many ancient artefacts; they might have been votive offerings from hoards buried here in prehistoric times, or they might date from a battle possibly fought here in AD 823 – well after the time of King Arthur – between the Saxons and the Cornish. Maybe Layamon was aware of the finds when he designated this site as the location of the Battle of Camlann. Certainly some Ordnance Survey maps from the nineteenth century had the words 'Battlefield, site of' marked in a field near Slaughterbridge, but the haziness of the history has meant that these designations no longer appear on current maps. And, indeed, even the name might be fake. 'Slaughterbridge' is suggestive of a bloody battle having been fought, but the name probably derives either from the nearby presence of a sloe tree or is a corruption of 'Sloven's Bridge', the former name for the settlement, which was recorded in a letter to the *Gentleman's Magazine* in May 1745 by a correspondent by the name of J. Pomeroy. The current name was possibly dreamed up to drum up tourism and help propagate the legend of this being the site of Arthur's famous battle.

Camelford itself, linked to Slaughterbridge by a narrow country road dense with trees, is an unremarkable sort of place. It's too large to be called a village and only the sparseness of the settlement all around it justifies it being called a town. On the Ordnance Survey map of Bodmin Moor it sits amid a rolling sea of contour lines on which bob villages and lonely farms linked by stringy, twisting country roads. It's the first place of any size on the River Camel and its modest new-build housing estates stretch like pulled elastic along the valley's gentle flanks. In his 1964 guide to Cornwall John Betjeman dismisses the place as a 'street of unpretentious grey slate houses [which] motor traffic today turns ... into a hell of a noise.' Well over fifty years later the traffic still grinds along Camelford's crooked and rising main street, but the town, though pleasant enough, has little to recommend it and certainly makes no effort to play on its Arthurian connections. Its position on the main A39 that runs through north Cornwall means that most visitors are just passing through, drawn by the more obvious appeal of Wadebridge and Padstow, a few miles further on along the road, or Tintagel, only a short drive along minor roads to the northwest.

If Camelford is barely a town, then Slaughterbridge is barely a hamlet. It comprises a skinny string of houses clinging to a country road that navigates a tight S-bend where it crosses the River Camel between Collan's Cross (on the A39) and the village of Delabole (famed for its wind farm). Here the river is just a narrow stream flowing through a claustrophobic valley that is secluded, thickly wooded – and secretive. Lying beside the river in a wooded glade, and reachable, since 2002, via a family-oriented concern calling itself the Arthurian Centre, is an extraordinary and very ancient 9 ft slab of stone decorated with mysterious inscriptions; and this, many claim, is the tombstone of King Arthur and a marker that commemorates the Battle of Camlann having been fought here. Its existence has been known about for centuries. Richard Carew wrote that 'the olde folke thereabouts will shew you a stone, bearing Arthur's name' – though in those days the stone was in a different location, standing upright in a field. (It later served as a footbridge until it was requisitioned to form the centrepiece of an eighteenth-century garden, complete with spiralling walkways and artificial cascades created in the river – an arcadian folly concocted by Charlotte Boscawen, who was Lady Falmouth of Worthyvale by dint of marrying into a wealthy and venerable Cornish family.)

The formal name for this slab of grey granite is the Worthyvale inscribed stone. It lies at the base of a vertical river cliff, nestling in a cove and resting on a scruffy patch of forest floor with its pointed end jutting out precariously over the river; there's no direct access to it, but it can be viewed from a specially-constructed platform at the top of the cliff. The stone is liberally caked in fluffy green moss (as is the dank cliff in whose shadow it lies), but the symbols written along its length are clear. They are not, however, readable, for although they look at first glance like letters – there's a 'T' clearly visible, and a backwards 'R' – they are in fact runic symbols, letter-like designs comprising lines and loops and curves. The stone is thought to be a monument from the early Christian era, fashioned possibly as early as the sixth century – the purported time of King Arthur. The runic symbols are written in Ogham, an alphabet that might have been developed by Irish druids as a means of making written communications that could be kept secret from the Romans – though other scholars support a later, Christian origin. Whatever its origins, Ogham flourished in the fifth and sixth centuries around the Irish Sea (most of the stones inscribed in Ogham have been found in Southern Ireland and in Pembrokeshire). The symbols on the Worthyvale Stone provide a translation of a faded Latin inscription that runs along another of the pillar's sides. Part of this inscription reads 'LATINI IC IACIT FILIUS MA ... RI' which can be translated as 'Of Latinus here lies the son of Macarus [or] Magarus' – though the middle letters of the second name are not readable because of damage to the stone, caused in all likelihood by its former use as a bridge. The link with Arthur is unfortunately extremely tenuous and stems from nothing more than the letters 'A' and 'R' being in close proximity. This has not, however, prevented the stone from becoming an established item of Arthuriana, and something of a tourist haunt. Alfred, Lord Tennyson, called by to see it in 1848, writing that it was difficult to locate but that he 'found it at last by a rock under two or three sycamores'. In 1893 a ticket office was built to collect monies from those who arrived by train when the railway station serving Camelford (on the now dismantled line to Wadebridge) was built just a short walk away from Slaughterbridge (though a fair distance from Camelford itself). Following surveys conducted in 2018 by the Cornwall Archaeology Unit it was found that the bank on which the stone is perched is actively eroding and the stone was therefore at risk, though at the time of writing its precise future was uncertain.

Right and below: The Worthyvale Inscribed Stone. (*Source, BabelStone, Wikimedia Commons*)

Excalibur and the Lady of the Lake

Dozmary Pool is not going to come high on the priority list of most tourists in Cornwall. It's set in a high, bleak, windswept and remote part of Bodmin Moor, just under 3 miles to the south of Bolventor, an unremarkable knot of houses that cluster around the Jamaica Inn, an ancient watering-hole made famous by Daphne du Maurier in her smuggling novel of the same name. In the past the inn has been a place of refuge for those crossing the often treacherous moor, and in February 2019 this role was revived when hundreds of drivers abandoned their cars on the nearby A30 during a severe snowstorm and occupied every nook and cranny of the place for the night. But nowadays the inn is rather commercialised, a spread of rooms that have an atmosphere no different to that of any other sizeable upmarket pub. The only things that distinguish it from establishments of similar size are the smugglers' knick-knacks that adorn the walls, the substantial gift shop at the back, and the adjacent museum dedicated to Daphne du Maurier and the history of smuggling on the moor. The inn does a brisk and efficient trade in catering for coach parties and trippers who turn off the A30 dual carriageway, the main road into and out of

Dozmary Pool on Bodmin Moor, a mysterious body of water that some claim is the home to the fabled Lady of the Lake. (*Andrew Beattie*)

Above and below: Dozmary Pool on Bodmin Moor, a mysterious body of water that some claim is the home to the fabled Lady of the Lake. (*Andrew Beattie*)

Dozmary Pool on Bodmin Moor, a mysterious body of water that some claim is the home to the fabled Lady of the Lake. (*Andrew Beattie*)

Cornwall, which runs just a few yards away; but the steady thrum of heavy traffic manages to sap away the last of anything that's left of Jamaica Inn's olde-worlde atmosphere.

From the road junction opposite the Inn a minor road heads south. Almost at once drivers leave Bolventor behind and find themselves driving through a featureless landscape of grazing land and scruffy marsh. After a mile or so the land on the right drops away to reveal what appears to be a small lake. This is, in fact, a remote tentacle of a very large body of water, Colliford Lake, a reservoir that on a map appears as an irregularly shaped ink blot, with its multiple arms curling and twisting in all directions. To the east of Colliford Lake – and not visible from its shores – is another, much smaller lake, a shallow and mysterious body of water that lies in a bowl in the low hills; and this is Dozmary Pool. At the pool's northern end are a couple of buildings – one an old farm, the other a much more modern residence – but there is no other sign of life. Grazing land stretches in all directions, to the brows of the low hills that flank the pool; it would be nice if it were possible to walk round it, but the sturdy fences render the reedy shore inaccessible. There are no tourist signs and no refreshment stalls, and the hum of traffic on the A30 over 2 miles away, indistinct but ever present, somehow accentuates the bleakness of the spot. Yet despite all this there is something mystical about this lonely lake, with its isolated setting on Bodmin Moor and its still, dark water. 'No streams feed it [and] no hills tower round it,' wrote John Betjeman in his 1964 *Shell Guide to Cornwall*. Yet Betjeman asserts that despite this, 'the uneventful expanse of peaty water, in its low heathery setting, has a brooding melancholy especially at evening.' Perhaps this sense of melancholy stems from the legends associated with the lake – such as the one that it is haunted by the ghost of Tregeagle, a wicked lawyer, who as penance for a dastardly deed was given the task of emptying the pool with a limpet shell. Another legend tells that it has no bottom, even though in 1859 and again in 1976 it dried up to reveal that actually it has. But the principal legend associated with Dozmary Pool is that it is the home of the fabled Lady of the Lake, who once entrusted the sword Excalibur to the young King Arthur, and who lifted her hand from the lake's surface once again to collect the sword when Sir Bedivere threw it back into the water after the king had fought his final battle.

The Lady of the Lake made her first appearance in Arthurian literature in Chrétien de Troyes' *Lancelot*. In this tale she appears as a fairy in a lake who brings up the tale's titular character when he is a child. Writers of the Vulgate Cycle were captivated, and quickly started using her in their tales. In the Lancelot-Grail cycle she is known as Viviane, a sorceress who entraps Merlin after he has become infatuated with her. In the post-Vulgate Cycles there are two ladies of the lake – the second one being Ninianne, who bestows the magical sword Excalibur on Arthur – and in an Italian tale, *Tavola Ritonda* (*The Round Table*), the Lady of the Lake is revealed to be a daughter of Uther Pendragon and therefore a sister of Arthur, and so villainous that Arthur vows to burn her. Thomas Malory keeps the tradition of two ladies in *Le Morte d'Arthur*. His description of Arthur being given the sword by the second lady (whom he names Nymue, though there are several variations of this name) opens with the king speaking with Merlin as they ride together through the countryside.

> Arthur said, 'I have no sword'. 'No force,' said Merlin, 'hereby is a sword that shall be yours.' So they rode till they came to a lake, which was a fair water and broad, and in the

midst of the lake Arthur was aware of an arm clothed in white samite, that held a fair sword in that hand. 'Lo!' said Merlin, 'yonder is that sword that I spake of'. With that they saw a damsel going upon the lake. 'What damsel is that?' said Arthur. 'That is the Lady of the Lake,' said Merlin; 'and within that lake is a rock, and therein is as fair a place as any on earth, and richly beseen; and this damsel will come to you anon, and then speak ye fair to her that she will give you that sword.' Anon withal came the damsel unto Arthur, and saluted him, and he her again. 'Damsel,' said Arthur, 'what sword is that, that yonder the arm holdeth above the water? I would it were mine, for I have no sword.' 'Sir Arthur, king,' said the damsel, 'that sword is mine, and if ye will give me a gift when I ask it you, ye shall have it.' 'By my faith,' said Arthur, 'I will give you what gift ye will ask.' 'Well!' said the damsel, 'go ye into yonder barge, and row yourself to the sword, and take it and the scabbard with you, and I will ask my gift when I see my time.' So Sir Arthur and Merlin alighted and tied their horses to two trees, and so they went into the ship, and when they came to the sword that the handheld, Sir Arthur took it up by the handles, and took it with him, and the arm and the hand went under the water.

Nymue makes a number of appearances in *Le Morte d'Arthur*, at Arthur's wedding and elsewhere, often aiding Arthur and his knights in their endeavours. As Arthur is dying of his wounds after the Battle of Camlann he asks one of his most trusted knights, Girflet, to complete a final task for him; that task is to return Excalibur to the Lady of the Lake. In his tale Malory substituted Girflet for the better-known Bedivere, who twice tries to cast the sword into the pond. He finally does so on the third attempt, when the still surface of the water is broken by the hand and arm of a woman who reaches out to catch the sword before returning it to the murky depths. The Lady of the Lake is subsequently presented as one of the magical queens who bear Arthur to Avalon.

The Lady of the Lake has become such an iconic figure in the Arthurian stories – as recognisable an image as Arthur drawing the sword from the stone – that any allusions to it in paintings or films or literature need no scene-setting or background explanation. Walter Scott wrote a poem about her in 1810, setting his story on Loch Katrine in the Trossachs in Scotland, and the poem became the basis of an opera by Rossini and songs by Schubert. In *Idylls of the King*, Tennyson once again splits the lady into two characters, one a deceitful enchantress, the other the benevolent keeper of Excalibur. In T.H. White's novel *The Once and Future King*, Merlin makes light of his imprisonment by her and even refers to it as a holiday. No wonder that the Monty Python comedy troupe were able to provide a very funny take on the story in their 1974 Arthurian parody *Monty Python and the Holy Grail*.

Unfortunately there are countless bodies of water spread through southwest England and Wales that claim to be the home of the Lady of the Lake. The Dozmary Pool's association with King Arthur and the fabled Lady seems to be based on nothing but the fact that it's a remote and mysterious body of water that's in the 'right' place for Arthurian legends – namely, eastern Cornwall. After all, the River Camel flows only a few miles to the west, on the fringes of Bodmin Moor, and places associated with Arthurian legends abound on the Moor, such as the prehistoric rock formation known as King Arthur's Halls. In 2018, when the appropriately (but coincidentally) named movie director Joe Cornish was shooting his film *The Kid Who Would Be King* in Cornwall, he made it clear in the film's publicity that the scenes he shot in the water tank at Leavesden Studios in Hertfordshire were meant to take place at the Dozmary Pool. The most remarkable aspect of the Dozmary Pool, however, is the archaeological evidence that it was once the site of rituals and ceremonies during which

The steamship Lady of the Lake on Loch Katrine in the Trossachs. The name of the ship is a reference to the poem by Sir Walter Scott, which sets the story of the Lady of the Lake on this Scottish loch. (*Source, John Darch, Wikimedia Copmmons*)

King Arthur's Hall, a Neolithic ceremonial site on Bodmin Moor. (*Source, Wikimedia Commons*)

time swords and other offerings were cast into the water. Some of these votive items have been unearthed from the lake shore by archaeologists. But in September 2017 a man from Doncaster and his young daughter made a truly unusual find. They uncovered a magnificent sword from the bottom of the lake – and wondered whether this could be *the* sword. The fantasy was punctured when a man from Plymouth claimed that he had purchased the 'fantasy sword' from a mail-order company in the late 1980s when he was 'very into spiritualism and the Celtic religion', and after a few drinks had often 'gone round knighting the people of Bodmin' with it. Then one day he decided to 'honour the legend' of Dozmary Pool by throwing the sword into it – so in the end the young girl's find wasn't quite as magical or historic as she'd hoped.

Glastonbury

Another body of water that might once have been home to Nimue is located in Somerset, at an ancient crossing point over the River Brue on the road that links the towns of Street and Glastonbury. In King Arthur's time the flat land hereabouts – the Somerset Levels – was a spongy morass of ponds and wetlands, a reminder of the distant days when the sea came this far inland (nowadays the coast is 15 miles away, at Burnham-on-Sea, where the Brue empties into the Bristol Channel). The span over the Brue was then known as the Pomparles Bridge, and beyond it was a sizeable lake – and it was into this lake, legend tells, that Sir Bedivere threw Excalibur after the Battle of Camlann. It can sometimes seem as if every body of water in western Britain was the home to the Lady of the Lake. But there are few who champion a lake beside the Brue as being home to Nimue; today, after all, there is no longer a lake here, and the bridge is a dull concrete affair from 1911 that replaced a venerable span from the Middle Ages. And really, the legend that the lake of Excalibur was once here is a sham, attaching itself to this part of Somerset on the back of other, more tangible Arthurian connections the area has – for just down the road from the Pomparles Bridge is Glastonbury Abbey, where King Arthur is supposed to have been buried and where some believe Holy Grail still lies waiting to be discovered. So in the end this place is just like the Dozmary Pool; Arthurian by association, riding on the coat tails of the more 'genuine' sites near by.

Glastonbury stands second only to Tintagel in geographical Arthuriana. Because of the discovery of the supposed grave and the legend that the Holy Grail was brought here and is buried here, King Arthur's spirit permeates the place. Yet unlike in Tintagel, where Arthur truly is king, in Glastonbury he often struggles to make his voice heard, for the town is a swirling stew of faiths and beliefs where new age hippies rub shoulders with Christian pilgrims and where witches and wiccans cheer on Hare Krishnas who regularly parade along the high street. The most notorious public exhibition of Glastonbury's 'alternative' culture is of course the music festival, held since 1970 at Worthy Farm in the village of Pilton, and now the largest open-air festival of performing arts in the world; there's dance, comedy, theatre, circus and cabaret alongside the headline music acts, the whole thing unfolding a good 8 miles east of Glastonbury (in fact Pilton is closer to the town of Shepton Mallet than Glastonbury, but maybe the 'Shepton Mallet Festival' lacked a certain cachet). The town has been attracting 'new age' evangelists since the nineteenth century. In 1934 the artist Katherine Maltwood gained a huge following when she suggested that a 'landscape zodiac' comprising a map of the stars on a gigantic scale and formed by features in the landscape such as roads, streams and field boundaries could be constructed over the surrounding countryside – and at its centre was Glastonbury. Her fanciful ideas were disproved by various surveys in the 1970s and 1980s. But still the new-agers and the pagans come. Among their places of veneration is the Chalice Well, a holy well set amid intimate gardens whose healing qualities have possibly been known about for millennia; it's a symbol of a 'female' deity that serves as a counterbalance to the male deity symbolised by the Tor, the great hill of resistant sandstone that rises ethereally from the surrounding marshes, crowned by a ruined church tower that is the iconic feature of the town. Yet Christianity retains a strong presence here too – and has done since the foundation of the abbey just after the time of King Arthur. Though the abbey is in ruins the place is still popular with pilgrims, with churches and meeting houses and a dedicated pilgrimage centre; in 1999 the charismatic Muslim spiritual leader Sheikh Nazim declared after a visit that, 'This is the spiritual heart of England … it is from here that the spiritual new age will begin and to here that Jesus will return.' No wonder the place features in so many novels, including Bernard Cornwell's popular *Warlord Chronicles*, a trilogy of books about Arthurian Britain.

The town – situated 23 miles south of Bristol, and with a population of just under 9,000 – has been inhabited since Neolithic times. Evidence has been found of Iron Age and Bronze Age settlement, but the early peoples who lived here fought a continuous battle with rising and falling sea levels, often retreating to seasonal camps on higher ground when the encroaching tides rendered them refugees. But the surrounding wetlands were also bountiful; reeds were harvested from swamps and roads were built with local timbers. In 1970 the so-called 'Sweet' Track was discovered west of the town, a timber trackway that was constructed in 3806/7 BC, the dating rendered so precise by scientific analysis of the timbers used. It is one of the oldest engineered roads known, and was named after its discoverer, local farmer Ray Sweet, who unearthed the ancient timbers while digging for peat. But Glastonbury's heyday came much later on, during the Dark Ages. In 658 the town fell into the hands of the Saxons following the Battle of Peonnum, and was absorbed into the Kingdom of Wessex. The precise date of the abbey's foundation is unknown but it was clearly flourishing when the Saxons arrived on the scene. They allowed the British abbot Bregored to remain in charge of his church, but when he died in 669 he was replaced by an Anglo Saxon, Berhtwald, and the abbey's rise to prominence as one of the most powerful and wealthy religious foundations in Anglo-Saxon England had begun. It was the Saxons who gave Glastonbury its name, too. To them the town was Glastingeburi – 'for in their tongue,' the historian Gerald of Wales later wrote, 'glas means glass, and a camp or town is called buri'. Gerald was referring to the glassworks that was operated by the abbey. But other suggestions have been put forward as to the derivation of the name. It might have been named after a legendary swineherder named Glas who was resurrected by St Patrick, or it could be a reference to a hovering mansion made of glass that was apparently seen floating above the Tor by St Collen, a local hermit. The chronicler William of Malmesbury, however, posited an entirely different origin; he claimed that the town was founded by and named after Glast, a descendent of Cunedda, a fifth-century ruler of northern Britain.

In 712 King Ine of Wessex enriched the endowment of Glastonbury Abbey and ordered a stone church to be built here to replace the original wooden one. The resulting church – the 'oldest I know of in England' according to William of Malmesbury – was enlarged in the 940s by the great monastic reformer St Dunstan, who later moved on from Glastonbury to become Archbishop of Canterbury. It was during Dunstan's time that a mile-long canal was built to link the abbey with the River Brue to allow easy exporting of the monastery's produce – grain, wine and fish. In the following century the church provided the setting for the coronation of Edmund Ironside, who succeeded Aethelred the Unready in 1016; when Edmund died less than a year later (to be succeeded by Canute) he was buried in the abbey in which he had been crowned. In 1086 the Domesday Book recorded the abbey to be the richest in the country, and around forty years later William of Malmesbury was commissioned to write a history of the monastery so that its monks could claim their institution had primacy over Westminster. William wrote of the 'stone pavement, the sides of the altar, and the altar itself [being] so loaded, above and below, with relics packed together that there is no path through the church, cemetery or cemetery chapel which is free from the ashes of the dead.'

Although the monastery was dissolved in 1539 its extensive ruins and peaceful grounds form a haven of peace away from Glastonbury's pagan, new-age noise. Many buildings scattered throughout the town owe their existence to the benevolence and wealth of the abbey and to the pilgrims that visited it.

They include the sizeable tithe barn that now houses the Somerset Rural Life Museum, and the George Hotel and Pilgrims Inn which, with its mullioned oriel windows and Plantagenet coat of arms above the wide doorway, remains a prominent feature along the High Street, where it jostles for position among the occult bookshops and vegan cafés advertising tarot readings. And although the abbey is now largely in ruins, it was this institution that gave the town its connection with King Arthur – because here, in 1191, the tomb of King Arthur was discovered in its grounds. Before this momentous discovery, the only connections Glastonbury had with King Arthur were tangential, and came in stories such as Caradoc of Llancarfan's account of the life of St Gildas, where the town features as the place where King Melwas has imprisoned Arthur's queen, Guinevere. According to Caradoc, Melwas had brought,

> her there because it was an impenetrable place, defended by reeds, rivers and marsh. The rebellious king [Arthur] had searched for the queen for a whole year, and had at last heard that she was there. At this news he raised the armies of all Cornwall and Devon, and the enemies prepared for war. Seeing this, the abbot of Glastonbury and his clergy and Gildas the wise went out between the battle lines and peaceably counselled Melwas the king to return the lady he had carried off. So she was returned, as she should have been, in peace and goodwill.

It seems hardly worth saying that, at the supposed time of King Arthur, Glastonbury Abbey didn't actually exist – so these events as described must be entirely fictitious.

The Tomb of King Arthur at Glastonbury Abbey

In his introduction to Thomas Malory's *Le Morte d'Arthur*, William Caxton discusses the notion as to whether King Arthur ever actually existed. 'Dyvers men holde oppynyon that there was no suche Arthur and that alle such books as been mad of hym ben but fayned and fables,' he wrote. However, he went on, 'there were many evydences of the contrarye', one of which was Arthur's 'sepulture in the monasterye of Glastyngburye'. This sepulchre (which Caxton had conceivably seen for himself) was a tomb that housed a collection of bones unearthed in the abbey churchyard in 1191, some three centuries before Caxton was writing. The said bones had been contained in three coffins, stacked one on top of the other in the ground. In the uppermost coffin were found the remains of a woman, her hair still intact; a skeleton of a man was found in the one below; while the lower of the three coffins was marked with the inscription in Latin: 'Here lies the famous King Arthur, buried in the Isle of Avalon'. We know these details from a chronicle written at the Margam Abbey near Port Talbot within a decade or so of the discovery at Glastonbury, by a writer who probably had before him a copy of a letter that the Glastonbury monks had sent out to announce their extraordinary find. The bones, the Margam chronicler recounts, were found to be 'sturdy enough and large,' and the monks 'transferred [them] with suitable honour and much pomp into a marble tomb in their church'. Were these the really the coffins of Guinevere, Mordred and Arthur? Or was this a stage-managed propaganda coup by members of a monastic community wanting to encourage pilgrims to come to their church so that they could raise money to pay for its reconstruction, after a disastrous fire in 1184, some seven years previously?

Gerald of Wales was given a detailed account of the discovery of the coffins by the abbot, Henry de Sully, on a visit he made to Glastonbury soon after the event. Not only was Gerald shown the lead cross that had marked Arthur's supposed coffin, he was also allowed to handle the huge thigh-bone that was said to be Arthur's, which 'when put next to the tallest man present, as the abbot showed us, and placed on the ground by his foot, reached three inches above his knee.' In addition, Gerald wrote in his *Liber de Principis instructione* that he considered Arthur's skull to,

> be of great, indeed prodigious, capacity, to the extent that the space between the brows and between the eyes was a palm's breadth. But in the skull there were ten or more wounds, which had all healed into scars with the exception of one, which made a great cleft, and seemed to have been the sole cause of death.

Gerald appears to have been convinced by what he saw.

> His body, for which popular stories have invented a fantastic ending, saying that it had been carried to a remote place, and was not subject to death, was found in our day in Glastonbury ... deep in the earth, enclosed in a hollow oak ... the discovery was accompanied by wonderful and almost miraculous signs.

147

Gerald also wrote of Guinevere's supposed remains, which included a 'golden tress of hair that belonged to a beautiful woman, in its pristine condition and colour, which, when a certain monk eagerly snatched it up, suddenly dissolved into dust.' Gerald surmised that the burial had taken place in secret, so that the Saxons 'against whom [Arthur] had fought with so much energy in his lifetime' would not discover it. For this reason the inscription on the lead cross 'was turned inwards to the stone, to conceal … what the coffin contained, and yet inform other centuries.'

The Margam chronicler maintains that the coffins were unearthed when a new grave was being dug for a recently deceased monk who had wanted to be buried in a specific part of the abbey churchyard. But Gerald of Wales, who was a royal courtier, maintained that the discovery apparently fulfilled a prophesy that King Henry II had 'heard from an aged British singer of stories that his [Arthur's] body would be found at least sixteen feet deep in the earth, not in a stone tomb, but in a hollow oak.' This led some to suggest that the discovery was stage managed and that the order to conduct such an elaborate hoax had come right from the very top. According to this particular medieval conspiracy theory, with Arthur's grave discovered Henry II would be able to denounce the claims of Welsh nationalists that Arthur would one day return and would rally them to victory against the English. The story is told in verse by Thomas Wharton in his poem *The Grave of King Arthur* (1777) in which a 'bard of aspect sage' exhorts Henry ''tis thine to save / From dark oblivion Arthur's grave!' – and the king resolves that he must indeed find it.

In 1278, nearly a century after the discovery of the bones, Glastonbury was visited by King Edward I and his queen, Eleanor. Edward, who built a fake round table at Windsor and might have been responsible for commissioning the famous one in Winchester, had a special reverence for King Arthur. During his visit the tomb was formally opened in front of the royal couple. The chronicler John of Glastonbury described how 'two separate chests,' were found therein, 'decorated with their portraits and arms'. The king's bones were 'of wonderful size,' he maintains, while those of the queen were 'of great beauty'. After inspection the bones were carefully wrapped in cloth and were placed in chests for formal reburial by the king and queen the next day in a specially constructed tomb – presumably a new one to replace the one that was described by the Margam Chronicle. 'They marked [the bones] with their seals and directed the tomb to be placed speedily before the high altar,' John went on, explaining that the heads and knee joints of both Arthur and Guinevere were buried in the tomb so that these objects could be venerated as relics by worshippers and pilgrims. It seems likely that on their visit, Edward and Eleanor were also shown the ornate cross that had been found with the coffins and had been described by Gerald of Wales as 'a leaden cross [that] was found laid under a stone, not above, as is the custom today, but rather fastened on beneath it.' Three centuries later this cross was seen by the antiquarian William Camden, who drew a sketch of it which he included in his 1610 work *Britannia*. Yet Camden's drawing shows that the cross bore a much simpler inscription to the one that had been copied down by Gerald of Wales. Camden's cross was inscribed with the words 'Here lies buried the famous King Arthur in the Isle of Avalon,' while Gerald's apparently also made mention of Guinevere. Either Gerald's account is unreliable or the cross drawn by Camden is wrong. Interestingly, in both accounts Arthur is described as a 'rex' – king – a title he never bore until literary works of the eleventh or twelfth century. This suggests that the Glastonbury cross – in whatever form it existed – was a fraud. But its precise story will never be known. Local tradition says that the cross survived the dissolution of the monastery but disappeared some time in the eighteenth century.

The tomb has not survived either. It was, however, an apparently glorious sight. Polydore Vergil, papal emissary to England during the reign of Henry VII and the writer of a history of England that was commissioned by Henry himself, called it a 'magnificent sepulchre'; a few years later Henry VIII's antiquarian John Leland described the tomb as being fashioned from black marble, with four lions at its base, a crucifix at the head and an image of Arthur carved in relief at the foot. It appears from this description that the design was based on classical sarcophagi, to stress the ancient lineage of Arthur. No one knows what happened to the coffins, the remains they contained or the tomb that housed them when the monastery was dissolved – or indeed what became of the abbey's dressed stone, bells, iron work and sculpture that was removed at that time and during later years. Today all that remains of the abbey are a melancholy assemblage of skeletal stone walls rising from carefully-tended lawns. One of the best-surviving parts of the abbey is the Lady Chapel, which began rising from the ashes of the original church almost immediately as the flames of the 1184 fire were extinguished, and whose finest element is an unfinished set of sculptures over the arched doorway showing the life of the Virgin Mary. The presumed location of Arthur's

Above: The remains of Glastonbury Abbey, once one of the richest in England.

Left: Glastonbury Abbey's Lady Chapel with its intricate carvings above the door. (*Andrew Beattie*)

tomb lies beyond the Lady Chapel between the extant walls of the nave of the church, which here form a mirror image, rising to roof height but tapering quickly on either side to enclose two arches. Between the walls a rectangular area of paving, grass growing through the cracks, stands next to a smaller rectangle of grass that is enclosed by a rim of stone. A sign informs us that,

> in the year 1191 the bodies of King Arthur and his queen were said to have been found on the south side of the Lady Chapel. On 19 April 1278 their remains were removed in the presence of King Edward I and Queen Eleanor to a marble tomb on this site. This tomb survived until the dissolution of the abbey in 1539.

No archaeologists have investigated the site of the tomb (which presumably was above ground – so actually there would be nothing to see if a dig were to take place). But the site of the supposed grave outside the walls of the Lady Chapel has been subject to a number of excavations. Here, in ground

The site of the supposed tomb of King Arthur, amidst the ruins of Glastonbury Abbey. (*Andrew Beattie*)

Left and below: The site of the supposed tomb of King Arthur, amidst the ruins of Glastonbury Abbey. (*Andrew Beattie*)

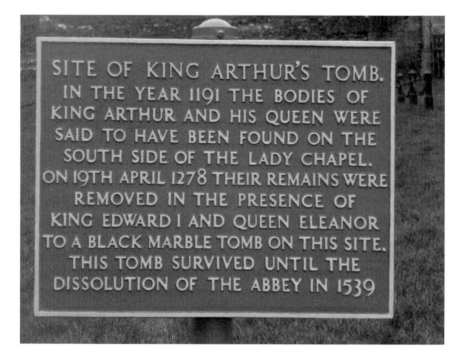

SITE OF KING ARTHUR'S TOMB.
IN THE YEAR 1191 THE BODIES OF
KING ARTHUR AND HIS QUEEN WERE
SAID TO HAVE BEEN FOUND ON THE
SOUTH SIDE OF THE LADY CHAPEL.
ON 19TH APRIL 1278 THEIR REMAINS WERE
REMOVED IN THE PRESENCE OF
KING EDWARD I AND QUEEN ELEANOR
TO A BLACK MARBLE TOMB ON THIS SITE.
THIS TOMB SURVIVED UNTIL THE
DISSOLUTION OF THE ABBEY IN 1539

Above and below: The site of the supposed original burial place of King Arthur, outside the walls of Glastonbury Abbey's Lady Chapel. (*Andrew Beattie*)

SITE OF THE ANCIENT GRAVEYARD WHERE IN 1191 THE MONKS DUG TO FIND THE TOMBS OF ARTHUR AND GUINEVERE

bumpy from all the digs and, before that, the burials that took place here, a sign poking out of the grass reads: 'site of the ancient graveyard where in 1191 the monks dug to find the tombs of Arthur and Guinevere'. In the 1960s Ralegh Radford turned his attention from Tintagel to Glastonbury and dug at this site. There was a clamour of excitement when he claimed to have found the two stone pyramids that Gerald of Wales claimed marked the grave, as well as the burial pit itself. In this pit Radford discovered chippings of stone from the abbey's own quarries at Doulting and surmised that this dated the pit to the 1190s, as he thought this type of stone was not used in the building of Glastonbury Abbey until the great reconstruction after the fire of 1184. However, Radford's conclusions have since been subject to some polite revision. It turns out that Doulting stone was used in all phases of the abbey's construction from Saxon times until the closure of the monastery in 1539. Moreover, beneath Radford's supposed burial pit a stone-cut cist grave from the tenth or eleventh centuries was discovered – clearly, it is not possible for a burial above this to be from an earlier date. Work continues on the site, most recently led by Professor Roberta Gilchrist of the University of Reading, who has discovered human remains from the late Middle Ages commensurate with the site's use as the abbey graveyard – but revealing nothing that might have linked the monastery with King Arthur. Yet Professor Gilchrist is wary of playing the role of the snooty academic, and of placing a wedge between her field of study and the convictions of those for whom the source of Glastonbury's spirituality rests partly on its identification as King Arthur's Avalon. 'We are not in the business of destroying people's beliefs,' she wrote. 'A thousand years of beliefs and legends are part of the intangible history of this remarkable place.'

Joseph of Arimathea, Glastonbury and the Holy Grail

The appearance of the Holy Grail in the stories of Arthur dates from almost exactly the same time as the king's burial place was supposedly discovered at Glastonbury. Readers first learned of the Grail in Chrétien de Troyes's final work *The Story of the Grail* (*Le Conte del Graal*), a poetic romance that was composed in around 1190. But the Grail plays only a minor role in the narrative, and it is not until line 3,208 of the poem that we finally encounter it, when the hero Perceval arrives at the castle of the

Fisher King – the last in a long line of rulers who are tasked with guarding the Holy Grail – and witnesses an extraordinary procession. It is headed by a squire bearing a white lance, from the tip of which blood trickles; he is followed by two young men carrying golden candelabras, and then by a beautiful girl, nobly attired, who bears a fabulously bejewelled vessel fashioned from pure gold in her hands. The assembled company sits down to a sumptuous meal served at a table of ebony and ivory, and Perceval thinks no more about the mysterious vessel until the following day when he leaves the castle and meets a maiden, his own cousin, who berates him for having asked no questions about it. The same rebuke comes his way when he reaches King Arthur's court – this time from the Loathly Damsel, who is described as an extraordinarily ugly maiden. Perceval commits himself to return to the castle of the Fisher King and ask about the Grail, but the narrative abruptly switches to the adventures of Sir Gawain, who heads off on a different quest entirely. Throughout his tale Chrétien uses the term 'graal' to describe the object seen in the procession; the assumption is that he means a shallow salver or bowl in which food is conveyed from the kitchen to the table in an aristocratic household. Some scholars have suggested that the origins of this mystical 'Grail' lie in vessels of plenty that feature in Celtic mythology, such as the life-restoring cauldron that Bran the Blessed possesses in the *Mabinogion*. Others have declared that the Grail makes its first appearance in the twelfth-century wall paintings found in churches in the Pyrenees depicting the Virgin Mary holding a bowl that radiates tongues of fire, which predate the Grail in Chrétien's tale by a number of decades.

That said, Chrétien's Grail appears to have no Christian context. That the Grail might be 'Holy' seems to be the invention of Robert de Boron, a knight and poet from Burgundy who developed the story of the Grail in his verse romance *Joseph d'Arimathie*, written just a few years after Chrétien's original story. In this tale Robert maintains that the Grail was the vessel used to serve wine at the Last Supper and which, later on, was used to collect the blood of Christ during the Crucifixion; in short it was the holiest relic in Christendom. That the Grail is linked with Joseph of Arimathea is also the invention of Robert de Boron. In the Bible Joseph is described as a wealthy but secretive follower of Jesus who asks permission from Pontius Pilate to bury the crucified Christ in what was originally intended to be his own tomb. In the centuries that followed a mass of legendary detail accumulated around Joseph, and Robert de

Boron expanded on these tales in his description of Joseph acquiring the holy vessel (from an apparition of Jesus) and travelling with it to Europe, where he founds a dynasty of Grail keepers.

It is unclear how, where and when the first stories emerged linking Glastonbury, the Holy Grail and Joseph of Arimathea; never before have the words 'legends lost in the mists of time' been so apposite. While Robert de Boron writes of how Joseph's followers bring the Grail to Britain, Joseph himself does not follow them (though in subsequent retellings of this story he does, and in the Lancelot-Grail cycle it is Joseph's son Josephus who brings the vessel – and with it Christianity – across the Channel). Somehow, in the years after the discovery of Arthur's grave, the stories of Joseph, the Grail and Glastonbury Abbey became conflated into a legend that Joseph had brought the vessel to Britain where he had lived in a hermitage beside the Chalice Well and founded the abbey as a repository for the sacred relic. This legend seems to have been intimately bound up in the discovery of King Arthur's supposed grave. In his *Deeds of the Kings of the English* of 1125 William of Malmesbury makes no mention of Joseph of Arimathea being the founder of the abbey. Instead he asserts that it was founded by preachers sent to Britain by Pope Eleuterus – though William also alleges that documents have been found pointing to Philip the Apostle as the founder. So it is clear that Joseph of Arimathea's name was not linked to the abbey at this time. Another of William's works, specifically on the history of the Abbey, has not survived in its original edition, though later additions have interpolations clearly added by Glastonbury monks (with an eye to enhancing the lucrative pilgrimage trade) that assert that Joseph of Arimathea was the founder. So it may be that the monks themselves were the propagators of the legend; as with the 'discovery' of Arthur's tomb, a canny monk might have spotted a marketing opportunity – and the community ran with it.

By the fourteenth century, spurred on by the efforts of the monks and the writings of Robert de Boron, Joseph of Arimathea had been firmly identified as the abbey's founder, and Glastonbury had been identified as the place where he had deposited the Holy Grail. One of the earliest writers to set these legends down on paper was John of Glastonbury, who in 1350 assembled a chronicle of the history of Glastonbury and wrote that Joseph, when he came to Britain, brought with him vessel containing the blood and sweat of Christ (without using the word Grail); he also came up with an inventive pedigree that demonstrated that King Arthur was Christ's direct descendant. A vital strand of the legend set down by John was that in former times the Somerset Levels would have been submerged and Joseph would have been able to reach Glastonbury Tor – then an island – by the same boat that had brought him all the way from Palestine. (A separate legend tells that when he was a boy, Jesus had had visited England with Joseph – a story told in William Blake's poem *Jerusalem*, the basis of the famous patriotic hymn, which asks 'And did those feet, in ancient times / Walk upon England's mountains green?' This legend, however, seems more linked with Cornwall than with Glastonbury, as it assumes that Joseph was a tin merchant and he was visiting his mines along with his young nephew.) According to the legends, the site of Joseph's original church in Glastonbury is now occupied by the abbey's Lady Chapel; as for the Holy Grail that Joseph buried somewhere near by – well, people are still looking for that – and as for Joseph's visit, that is still commemorated in Glastonbury through the famous legend of the Glastonbury thorn. It is said that when Joseph disembarked at Glastonbury he stuck his staff into the ground and it immediately flowered into a hawthorn tree – the famous Glastonbury thorn that flowers twice annually, once in the spring and again at Christmas. The original thorn was revered by pilgrims in the Middle Ages but was cut down during the English Civil War. In 1951 a replacement was planted on Wearyall Hill, which overlooks the town, and every year a sprig is cut from the tree by the local Anglican vicar and the eldest child from the town's St John's School – and sent to the queen. Unfortunately the tree on Wearyall Hill was vandalised in 2014, though a new one has since been planted in its place.

In the late nineteenth century the legend of Joseph, the Grail and Glastonbury was revived and strengthened further, inspired by a rekindled interest in Arthuriana and by spiritual movements that centred on ancient sites. The association remains strong, despite 'competition' from Rosslyn Chapel near Edinburgh, which emerged in the mid-twentieth century as the supposed place where the Holy Grail was hidden – though in this case the Grail is not a physical relic but a symbol of secret knowledge deposited in the chapel by the Knights Templar. Such flights of fancy are part of a vast, contemporary 'Grail' industry that has variously captivated the Nazis, conspiracy theorists and writers of popular fiction, among others – and which have largely ignored Glastonbury, and to some extent King Arthur too, leaving the Grail legends here to be curated by the more benign group of new age thinkers and pagans who venerate the stories of King Arthur and the Holy Grail alongside other aspects of spiritualism and magic. (Glastonbury's new age outlook has even affected the history of the Abbey; in 1919 the Glastonbury Abbey Trust had to dismiss the archaeologist Frederick Bligh Bond after he revealed that he had made many of his interpretations of his finds in collaboration with a psychic medium.) This remarkable miasma of legend, pagan mythology and Christianity is seen nowhere else in Britain, and is celebrated most famously in John Cowper Powys's epic and multi-layered 1932 novel *A Glastonbury Romance*.

The richness of Powys's novel is testament to Glastonbury's role as a keeper of age-old mysteries. With its bead shops and posted flyers with promises of rune reading, spiritual healing and the like, and its ability to draw in new-age drifters by the tent-load, Glastonbury is certainly one of the most unusual places in Britain to spend a couple of hours – though for those who are not 'believers' in whatever belief system Glastonbury is proselytising, that's probably long enough. The best view over the town is from the famous Tor, a conical hill of sandstone that rises above Glastonbury's western fringes and whose distinctive, boxy tower ensures that it can be identified from tens of miles away – even from the coast

The spirit of King Arthur permeates the town of Glastonbury. (*Andrew Beattie*)

Above and right:
Glastonbury Tor, with its
ruined church tower, is
one of the most famous
landmarks in Southwest
England. (*Andrew Beattie*)

of South Wales, with the Bristol Channel and the marshy flatness of the Somerset Levels ensuring uninterrupted sightlines. The tower (now open to the sky) is all that remains of the fourteenth-century church of St Michael that stood here in the Middle Ages; the rest of the church was destroyed in September 1539, when Thomas Cromwell's commissioners arrived without warning to dissolve the small monastic community that made its home on the Tor. Just two months later Richard Whiting, the abbot of Glastonbury Abbey, was hanged, drawn and quartered at the summit of the Tor after he resisted Thomas Cromwell's commissioners who had come to close down his abbey. Glastonbury Tor is, in fact, one of a number of protuberances that rise above the spongy Levels – though with its tower and profile it is easily the most recognisable and the most iconic. The summit is 158 metres above sea level and it's easy to appreciate that the Tor was once an island, with seawater lapping up against its lower flanks. In the winter the mysterious levels, with their open fields of grass fringed by drainage ditches and arrow-straight country roads, is still flooded – and the low-lying damp ground can produce a visual effect known as a 'Fata Morgana', which is best viewed from the summit of the Tor. It is an optical phenomenon in which rays of light are bent as they move through air whose lower layers are cold but whose upper layers have become warmed; it is seen nowhere else in Britain and its name is derived from Morgan le Fay, the powerful sorceress who was the antagonist of King Arthur.

Part Three

A GAZETTEER OF ARTHURIAN SITES

Arthurian Sites in Cornwall

Bossiney

Bossiney comprises a cluster of cottages and holiday homes adjoining Tintagel village. The mound at its centre was once the site of a castle and is the setting for a legend involving the Round Table (see p.65–66).

Camelford

Inland from Tintagel, this small town has been claimed as the original site for both Camelot and Arthur's last battle at Camlann (see p.125 and 130 onwards).

Castle-an-Dinas

This hill-fort a few miles inland from Newquay has been equated with Damelioc, where the warlord Gorlois holed himself up while being pursued by the armies of Arthur's father, Uther Pendragon. According to legend this was also Arthur's hunting lodge (See p.63–64).

Castle Dore and the Tristan Stone

The tale of the lovers Tristan and Iseult originated as a standalone tale that writers in the Middle Ages later wove into the Arthurian canon by making Tristan a knight of the Round Table. It has always been associated with Cornwall. In a version by the Norman-French poet Béroul, the fortress of King Mark, Tristan's uncle (Mark is Tristan's father in some versions of the story), is located at 'Lancien', which some have said equates with the farm at Lantian, outside Golant on the Fowey estuary in the southwest of the county (another farm nearby, Kilmarth, translates as 'Mark's Retreat').

The archaeologist Ralegh Radford, who worked extensively at Tintagel, believed that Castle Dore, an Iron Age fort near Lancien, was the actual site of Mark's fortress. Today all that can be seen there are 7-ft-high earthworks, though post-holes uncovered during archaeological excavations suggest that there were more substantial timber buildings here at one time, including two grand halls. The novelist Daphne du Maurier, who developed a long association with Cornwall, had a particular affinity for Castle Dore. In the mid 1960s she wrote of the 'tumbling earth and the brambled ditch' that characterised the site. 'All is buried now,' she continued. 'Stables, granaries, porters' lodges, chieftain's hall lie confused and intermingled with the huts of the Iron Age settlers.' Nearby, at the side of the road between Castle Dore and Fowey, is a tall, slender standing stone, the Tristan Stone, which was moved to this location in 1971. The stone is 7-ft tall and is inscribed in Latin with the words 'Here lies Drustanus, son of Cumnomorus'; Drustanus is an early form of the name 'Tristan' while Cumnomorus is the name by which Mark is sometimes known.

The Tristan Stone. (*Source, Rod Allday, Wikimedia Commons*)

Condolden Barrow

This is a prehistoric barrow situated at the summit (308 metres) of a hill that rises just over 2 miles east-south-east of Tintagel village. Access is from a minor road nearby. The barrow is supposedly the burial place of Cado, the guardian of Guinevere.

Dozmary Pool

Situated near the Jamaica Inn pub, this pool in a remote part of Bodmin Moor is supposedly home to the Lady of the Lake (see p.136 onwards).

Kelly Rounds

Also known as Castle Killibury, this Iron Age hill-fort just outside Wadebridge might have been the location of Arthur's court (discussed on p.91).

King Arthur's Hall

Situated in a remote, marshy, gently undulating part of Bodmin Moor named King Arthur's Downs, this is an impressive arrangement of standing stones from the prehistoric era. There's no road access; expect a walk of around 2½ miles, along a footpath that starts as a track just west of Penwood House, east of St Breward.

Lanyon Quoit

This impressive dolmen, consisting of a slab of rock supported by three pillars, is situated near Penzance and is easily accessible from the Madron to Morvah road. It was re-erected in the nineteenth century, and local lore tells that it's high enough for a man on horseback to shelter beneath. Inevitably, a number of Arthurian legends have become attached to it – such as the story that Arthur stopped here for a bite to eat on the way to his last battle, and Merlin prophesied that Arthur and his knights would meet up here at the end of the world.

Loe Pool

Loe Pool is a lagoon cut off from the open sea by Loe Bar, a ridge of sand and shingle that extends from the seaside town of Porthleven across Mount's Bay in Southwest Cornwall. The pool is one of a number of sites that have been claimed as the pool from which the Lady of the Lake emerged to give

Loe Pool in Cornwall, a contender for being the home to the Lady of the Lake. (*Source, Rod Allday, Wikimedia Commons*)

Arthur his sword, Excalibur (Alfred, Lord Tennyson believed this to be the 'true' pool of the Lady of the Lake). More 'visitor friendly' than the Dozmary Pool, Loe Pool has a path running around its perimeter.

Slaughterbridge

This hamlet just north of Camelford is home to the Worthyvale Inscribed Stone, which according to tradition marked the site of the Battle of Camlann and was Arthur's tombstone (see p.133-4).

St Dennis

Along with the Kelly Rounds this village also lays claim to being Damelioc, the site of Gorlois's fortress and Arthur's hunting lodge (covered on p.64).

St Michael's Mount

This striking rocky island is one of the most iconic images of Cornwall. Situated just off the county's south coast, just east of Penzance, the place has been a holy site since the fifth century, when St Michael appeared to some local fishermen. In the twelfth century the mount was granted to the monks of the abbey on the remarkably similar-looking Mont St Michel

St Michael's Mount in Cornwall, where Arthur fought the giant Cormoran. (*Source, Wkimedia Commons*)

in Brittany, and a Benedictine Priory was situated here until 1424. In Arthurian legend the mount is the stronghold of a giant named Cormoran, whom Arthur engaged in battle. The castle (which dates from the late Middle Ages) is also considered to be one of the 'Grail' castles – that is, castles that have at one time served as the repository for the Holy Grail.

St Nectan's Glen

Just over a mile due east of Tintagel, this secluded, verdant glen winds up from the coast to a splashing waterfall and secluded pool (the latter known as St Nectan's kieve) that was once, reputedly, the home of a reclusive saint named Nectan, the brother of St Morwenna. Nectan established his hermitage here in the sixth century and during stormy weather he would walk down the river to the mouth of a narrow inlet known as Rocky Valley where he would ring a bell to warn ships of the nearby rocks. Legend tells that the end of his life, realising that he was about to die, Nectan took the silver bell from the chapel and dropped it through a rift in the rock, far out of sight; he then died and the waterfall diverted itself so that it flowed over his grave. Some time later a group of miners came looking for the bell but abandoned the quest when they heard a ghostly ringing sound, accompanied by a child's voice that chimed 'the child is not born who shall recover this treasure'. Today the kieve is decked out with ribbons, photographs and crystals, and small piles of rocks known as 'fairy stones'. The place is popular with families and is reached by a mile-long walk from a car park on the main Tintagel to Boscastle coast road. Arthurian connections are slight but somehow, in this part of the world, somewhat inevitable; it seems that according to local legend Arthur and his knights gathered here before embarking on their quest for the Holy Grail, and prepared themselves spiritually by bathing in the glen's sacred waters. In 1910 Charles G. Harper observed in his guide to the coast of North Cornwall that 'the romance of this lovely waterfall is perhaps a little obscured by the necessity for applying at Trethevy Farm for the key'. Nowadays walkers who reach this tranquil spot via the path from Trethevy will find that there's a ticket office and a café – and no need to call in at the farm.

St Nectan's kieve, a waterfall in a secluded glen near Tintagel to which a number of Arthurian legends have become attached. (*Andrew Beattie*)

Tintagel

The supposed site of Arthur's conception and birth – a tradition established by the twelfth-century historian, Geoffrey of Monmouth (covered on p.47 onwards).

Tregeare Rounds

Situated close to Pendogget, a few miles east of Polzeath, this is a third contender for Gorlois's fort at Damelioc (covered on p.64).

Trethevy Quoit

Trethevy Quoit, sometimes called Arthur's Quoit, and known locally as the 'Giant's House', is a megalithic burial chamber dating back to the second millennium BC. It is situated a mile north of Liskeard in southeast Cornwall, near St Cleer, and comprises an impressive dolmen consisting of a giant sloping slab supported by a tight cluster of upright stones. The capstone is punctured by a natural hole which was possibly used for astronomic observations. Legends say that the quoit was covered with a mound and that locals thought it was a 'fairy hill' – which is why the name of Arthur, who was well known to have links with the fairy folk, is associated with it.

Arthurian Sites in Somerset, Dorset, Wiltshire, Hampshire and Bath

Amesbury

Archaeological excavations have found proof that the site of Amesbury, near Stonehenge, was occupied as far back as 8000 BC, making it one of the oldest settlements in Britain. It was first associated with Arthurian legend in Malory's *Morte d'Arthur*. According to Malory, when Arthur died, Guinevere retreated to a convent in Amesbury, where she turned to a life of fasting, prayer and penance – most likely in atonement for her actions in her husband's court. Lancelot, her former lover, came to the abbey to see her, but she refused him. When she finally died it was Lancelot who returned for her body and arranged for her to be buried beside Arthur at Glastonbury – a final act of penance. When Malory was writing his tale it seems that Amesbury was fairly well known for being a retreat for noble and royal women, such as Eleanor of Provence, who moved to the abbey twelve years after the death of her husband Henry III.

Badbury Rings

This Iron Age hill-fort in Dorset is one of the claimants to be the site of Mount Badon, Arthur's greatest battle. Situated beside an old Roman road, the Rings consist of a triple rampart construction; there are traces of occupation from the sixth century, but the main link with Arthur's battle is simply the name.

Brent Knoll

This iconic hill rises on the northwestern edge of the Somerset Levels and (famously) overlooks Sedgemoor Services on the M5 motorway, at the halfway point between Bristol and Taunton. The summit is accessed from a path (it's a 20 minute walk) that begins beside the church in Brent Knoll village. From the summit the views yawn out to encompass Glastonbury Tor in one direction, and the Bristol Channel in the other. Humps and

Looking across the Somerset Levels towards Glastonbury Tor from the summit of Brent Knoll. (*Andrew Beattie*)

The Iron Age defences at Brent Knoll, a contender for being the site of Badon, where Arthur secured his most historic victory. (*Andrew Beattie*)

bumps scattered across the extensive summit are remnants of defences established here from Roman times to the Middle Ages. According to legend Arthur sent a young hopeful named Yder to prove himself against three giants here; Yder slays the giants but is killed in the encounter. By way of atonement Arthur asks eighty monks in Glastonbury to pray for Yder's soul, and gives the land around Brent Knoll to Glastonbury Abbey. Although this story appears in editions of William of Malmesbury's *The Antiquities of Glastonbury*, it is thought that it was added some time after the original edition (dating to the early twelfth century) to prove that the abbey had held the land around Brent Knoll for centuries. The story probably derives from Welsh folklore, with the figure of Arthur grafted onto it in the Middle Ages. A separate legend suggests that this is the site of the Battle of Badon.

Cadbury Castle

This Iron Age hill-fort near Yeovil was for a time considered by leading archaeologists to be the site of Camelot (discussed on p.116 onwards).

Glastonbury

This small town south of Bristol, overlooked by its iconic tor, is reputedly the burial place of King Arthur and was where Joseph of Arimathea deposited the Holy Grail (covered on p.142 onwards).

Liddington Castle

This Bronze Age hill-fort in Wiltshire lies at an altitude of 277 metres and is close to the ancient long-distance track known as the Ridgeway. Occupation of the fort dates back to the seventh-century BC, and it is another of the many contenders for the site of Mount Badon.

Little Solsbury Hill

Geoffrey of Monmouth equated Mount Badon with Bath, and indeed a thirteenth-century edition of the *Historia Brittonum* persevered at Cambridge explains that the battle was fought 'where the Baths of Badon are' – and this has been seized on by writers who claim that one of the hills above the city of Bath is the former battle site. Badon was the name given by the Anglo Saxons to Bath (Baden meaning 'bath' in modern-day German – hence Baden Baden) and it appears that Geoffrey simply picked Bath as the location for Mount Badon for these reasons. Little Solsbury Hill is a hill that overlooks the city from a height of just over 200 metres, and at the top is an Iron Age hill-fort, occupied until around 100 BC – but, as usual, nothing more than anecdotal evidence links the place to King Arthur. Glastonbury is just 23 miles away so the hill is definitely in the 'right place' for somewhere with an Arthurian heritage. The hill can be reached via a minor road that leads up to it from the village of Batheaston; nothing is made of the hill's Arthurian connections and the place seems known only to locals as a blustery site for jogging and dog-walking.

Stonehenge

According to Arthurian tradition, this monument was built by Merlin as the tomb for Aurelius, Arthur's uncle; contemporary pagan celebration of the monument has also embraced the King Arthur legend. (Covered on p.61-62)

Winchester

According to medieval tradition this was the site of Camelot (see p.94 onwards).

Arthurian Sites in Wales and the Welsh Borders

Arthur's Cave

This cave near Monmouth is situated at the foot of Little Doward Hill, and was probably occupied in earliest times. Legend tells that Arthur hid some treasure here and Merlin blessed the cave to make sure the treasure stayed hidden.

Arthur's Quoit

This rock formation is situated close to St David's Head in Pembrokeshire and is known in Welsh as *Coetan Arthur*. It is a prehistoric rock formation from around 3000 BC, with an enormous metre-thick capstone covering a high chamber partly dug into the rock. Arthur's name has become attached to this and other similar features through his early depiction as a giant who was given to throwing rocks around when he was angry.

Arthur's Stone (Dorstone)

Taking the form of an enormous slab of rock supported by curved boulders, this Neolithic burial chamber at Dorstone in Herefordshire dates back 5,000 years. According to legend this was the place where Arthur slew a giant and buried it afterwards.

Arthur's Stone (Maen Ceti)

Situated on Cefn Bryn Common, on one of the highest points of the Gower Peninsula, this chambered cairn was supposedly a stone that Arthur, the giant, found in his shoe, and bad-temperedly threw aside. It stands prominent in a level landscape of tall grasses and consists of a large, blocky boulder supported by smaller upstanding rocks.

The Berth, Shropshire

The Berth is a prehistoric hill-fort near Baschurch in Shropshire; adjacent to it is a pool named Berth Pool. The fact that the Berth was once surrounded by water has led author Graham Phillips to assert that this is Avalon, the burial place of King Arthur. Part of Phillips's 'evidence' is that Malory named the boat that carried Arthur away a 'barge', which suggests not a seafaring vessel but one that might cross an inland waterway such as a lake. Lilly Chitty, an archeologist working here in 1925, heard a local legend that 'a prince was buried beneath a mound on the south slope after a great battle and that his men were buried in a longer, narrower mound nearby' – while the *Canu Heledd*, a poem in the *Red Book of Hergest*, a collection of Welsh poems compiled around 1400, identifies the area around modern day Baschurch as the burial site of the seventh-century kings of Powys. A first-century cauldron – an object that held religious significance then – was discovered in 1906 in a stream draining Berth Pool, which suggests that religious offerings were once cast into the water. However, Avalon was a construct from the 1130s, thought up by Geoffrey of Monmouth, and it must be said that another poet of the same era, Layamon, specifically wrote that Arthur was taken away by sea rather than by river barge – he narrates how 'there came moving in from the sea a small boat, driven onwards by the waves'.

Bosherston Lily Ponds

Bosherston Lily Ponds in Pembrokeshire is a freshwater lake that lays claim to being the home of the Lady of the Lake and Excalibur.

Caerleon

This small town near Newport in South Wales is considered by many to be the possible site of Camelot (See p.104 onwards).

Caerwent

Just east of Caerleon, this village is blessed with a number of monuments from Roman times, most particularly its walls, which are some of the best-preserved anywhere. Caerwent, like Caerleon, is a possible contender for being the site of Camelot (See p.113-6).

Camlan

This small village is located in the Dovey valley and lies on a trio of natural routeways leading to Bala, Dolgellau and Powys. Could this have been the site of the Battle of Camlann, at which Arthur was mortally wounded?

Carn Gafallt

Mentioned in the ninth-century *Mirabilia* as a stone cairn in which is imprinted the pawprint of Arthur's dog; situated in wild countryside in east-central Wales (covered on p.42-43).

Castle Dinas Bran

Towering above the Dee Valley in the Vale of Llangollen, this gloomy castle on an isolated rock pinnacle was built in the thirteenth century on the site of an Iron Age fort. A legend tells that the castle was once the home of Bran the Blessed, a pagan Welsh God, who might have been the model for the Fisher King. An obscure and somewhat convoluted legend maintains that Merlin once hid a golden harp here, which can only be found by a blue-eyed boy with yellow hair who owns a white dog with a silver eye.

Cerrig Meibion Arthur

This pair of standing stones in the Preseli Hills in Pembrokeshire, situated near Cwm Garw farm, are also known as the Stones of Arthur's Sons or Tŷ Newydd. They date back to the second millennium BC and are situated in a rough area of moorland and marsh. According to tradition the stones mark the place where Amr and Lohot, the sons of Arthur, were killed by the boar, Twrch Trwyth.

Craig y Ddinas

Craig y Ddinas (Dinas Rock) is a high limestone promontory on the southern fringe of the Brecon Beacons that is riddled with caves (the area is popular with cavers, climbers and adventure sports enthusiasts). A tale relates that on London Bridge a Welshman with a hazel walking stick meets a wise man, who persuades him that together they must visit the place where the hazel was cut, as treasure lies hidden there. They travel to Dinas Rock and find the tree from which the hazel was cut, and enter a cave beneath it. In the cave is a bell which the wise man says on account be touched – because if it rings the warriors in the cave will awake and ask 'Is it day?', for which the answer must be 'no, sleep thou on'. The pair successfully enter the cave and take some of the treasure, and when the bell is accidentally touched, the Welshman gives the correct answer. However on the next occasion when the Welshman enters the cave, this time without the wise man, he again accidentally rings the bell, and forgets the answer he must give. Arthur and his warriors then rise up and attack him; he flees and is never able to find the entrance to the cave again.

Din Sylwy

This flat-topped limestone hill in Anglesey is also known as Bwrdd Arthur (meaning 'Arthur's Table'). It is known for its fantastic coastal views. The origins of the name are obscure, though it might have been that the fort was known as a formal meeting place, which later became equated with the Round Table around which Arthur's knights gathered.

Ffynnon Cegin Arthur

The name of this curative spring, located in a forest near Llanddeiniolen in Gwynedd, translates as the 'well of Arthur's kitchen'; the spring has long had pagan and druidical associations.

Gamber Head

The source of the River Gamber near Wormelow in Herefordshire, and the adjacent tomb of Arthur's son Amr, are mentioned in the ninth-century *Mirabilia* as being sites with an Arthurian connection (see p.42).

Llyn Ogwen

Llyn Ogwen is a lake in Snowdonia situated 310 metres above sea level; here Nimue, the Lady of the Lake, apparently makes her home beneath its surface.

Ogmore Castle

This medieval castle is situated just south of Bridgend, mid-way between Cardiff and Swansea. It was built to guard a major crossing point into South Wales and stands alongside the River Ewenny. The earliest parts of the castle were built by William de Londres in the twelfth century. The link to Arthur is through the famous 'Arthur Stone', discovered by accident in the cellars where it was being used as a paving stone. An inscription on the stone reads: 'Be it known to all that Arthmail (Arthur) has given this field to God, to Glywyn [Arthur's cousin and the brother of St Cadoc] and to Nertat and to Bishop Fili [after whom Caerphilly is named]'. The stone is now on display in the St Fagans National Museum of History in Cardiff.

Ogof Arthur

This legendary cave on the southwestern coast of Anglesey may not actually exist! It is either accessed from the shore or through a secret

Ogmore Castle in South Wales, where the famed 'Arthur Stone' was discovered in the cellars. (*Source, Wikimedia Commons*)

entrance in the burial chamber of Barclodiad-y-Gawres on the cliffs above. The cave is rumoured to stretch for a mile inland. It was in this cave that Arthur sought shelter during a battle with Irish pirates, and also where he hid all his treasure.

Pentre Ifan

This Bronze Age burial chamber in the Preseli Mountains is around 3,000 years old. The stories connected with it date back to the era when Arthur was supposed to be a giant. According to local tradition Arthur threw or dropped the huge stones, which now form a perfect formation with pointed boulders forming the 'legs' of a table and a huge slab lying horizontally between them.

Pen-y-Fan

This mountain in the Brecon Beacons is thought to be the peak that Gerald of Wales named Kaerarthur, which he translated as 'Arthur's Seat'.

Ruthin

Ruthin is a small market town in northeast Wales. On the west side of its main marketplace, St Peter's Square, a badly weathered slab of sandstone some 1.2 metres long, 0.6 metres high and 0.6 metres wide sits behind a protective grille. A plaque above explains the significance of the rock, which is named Maen Huail, 'on which tradition states King Arthur beheaded Huail, brother of Gildas the historian'. A second plaque, added by the Welsh heritage body CADW, states that Gildas was Arthur's 'rival, in love and war'. The names and events described are taken from an obscure chronicle written by Elis Gruffudd, a member of the Calais garrison during the reign of Henry VIII, and who was from nearby Llanasa, in Flintshire. Huail, the older brother of Gildas, is identified as an adversary of Arthur in the much earlier *Life of Gildas*, but Gruffud's tale is his own, derived either from his imagination or from a local folkloric tale about a different figure named Huail. He describes how a quarrel erupts between the 'cheeky and wanton' Huail, son of Caw o Brydain, the ruler of Edeyrnion, and King Arthur, over one of Arthur's mistresses. A fight ensues and Arthur is wounded in the knee, leaving him lame. The two negotiate a peace in which Huail must never again refer to the king's injury. When Huail sees Arthur in Ruthin dressed in women's clothes and dancing with a group of girls he comments that Arthur would be a good dancer were it not for his wounded knee. Arthur overhears him, and has Huail brought before him in the town of Caerwys; he then orders him to be beheaded over a stone in Ruthin's market place. However, Arthur has no other connection with Ruthin, whose market place wasn't laid out until the late thirteenth century, while Gruffud probably chose Caerwys as Arthur's seat of justice because in his day it hosted the assizes court. The habit of local storytellers blending the legends of King Arthur with local tales and geography in this manner was common during the Middle Ages.

St Govan's Chapel

This tiny chapel, situated in a cleft in the rocks on the southernmost part of the Pembrokeshire coast, is only accessible via a flight of steps cut into the cliff. It dates to the thirteenth century but is built on the site of a sixth-century chapel whose seat and altar, hewn from the rock, are still visible. According to local legend St Govan was really Sir Gawain, and he came here after Arthur's last battle to live out his days as a hermit. It is also said that he lies buried beneath the altar.

Arthurian Sites in Northern England and Scotland

The possibility that King Arthur (or his legend) might hail from the north – the Arthur of *Y Gododdin* and Admonan's *Life of St Columba* – is discussed in Part One of this book. Some sites in Scotland that are known as 'Arthurian' might actually be related to the Clan Arthur, a subgroup of the Campbell clan, or alternatively might derive their name from other historic or folkloric figures named Arthur. The most famous incidence of this is Arthur's Seat, a gnarled lump of extinct volcano that rises above Edinburgh, which is probably named after a local hero named Arthur, rather than the king.

Camboglanna Roman Fort (Birdoswald)

This fort at the western end of Hadrian's Wall sits on an escarpment overlooking the Irthing Valley, near Gilsand in Cumbria. Some believe this place to be the site of Camlann or Camelot – but only the first syllable of the name provides any 'evidence', and the Roman-period name was unlikely to have been used in the Middle Ages when the idea of Camelot originated.

Camelon

This village near Falkirk is yet another contender for Camelot and Camlann – once again only the similarity of the names provides the possible link. In Roman times a fort was located here, close to the Antonine Wall.

Carlisle

Although it is tempting to think that the 'northern' King Arthur died out some time in the Dark Ages, to be usurped by the more familiar Welsh or Cornish Arthur, this is not the case. The most significant appearance of a 'northern' Arthur comes in *The Awntyrs off Arthure at the Terne Wathelyne* (*The Adventures of Arthur at Tarn Wadling*), whose composition can be dated to around 1400, and whose author was probably a Carlisle-based cleric. Given the similarity of its name with Camelot and, particularly, with Caerleon in South Wales, Carlisle (known in the poem as Carlele) is a contender for the location of both Arthur's fabled palace and his last battle, at Camlann. The work is written in alliterative verse and opens with Arthur's court riding out to a hunt in Inglewood Forest, which is south of Carlisle. At a lake known as Tarn Wadling, Gawain and Guinevere encounter a hideous ghost who reveals that she is Guinevere's mother,

177

condemned to suffer for the sins of adultery that she committed while alive. The second half of the poem recounts a conflict between a knight, Sir Galeron of Galloway, and Sir Gawain. Inglewood Forest today consists of a patchwork of woodlands spread between Carlisle and Penrith; Tarn Wadling was drained in the nineteenth century and is now little more than a depression covered by trees.

Drumelzier

This small town in the Scottish Borders is known for its connections with Merlin, who according to local legend prophesied that he would be cudgelled, pierced, and drowned – which indeed happened when he was beaten by the shepherds of King Meldred, which caused him to fall into the River Tweed where he was impaled by a stake in the water. Merlin's grave is today modestly marked by a thorn tree near where the Pausayl burn meets the River Tweed. The tree is surrounded by an enclosure and marked with a plaque. The church in the village of Stobo, close by, has a contemporary stained glass window depicting Merlin kneeling before Saint Kentigern, who converted him to Christianity.

Dumbarton Rock

This rocky peninsula overlooks the River Clyde at Dumbarton, west of Glasgow; the name originates from the Gaelic *Dun Breatann*, meaning Fort of the Britons, and is mentioned by Geoffrey of Monmouth, who records the legend that Arthur left Hoel of Brittany, his sick nephew, here while on campaign. Hoel made a full recovery, but was besieged in the castle by the Scots and Picts. The rock is a distinctive landmark with two peaks and was an important military stronghold during the Dark Ages. Another legend associates Dumbarton Rock with Merlin, who stayed for a time in the court of Rhydderych Hael, a ruler of Dumbarton. For seven hundred years the rock has been the site of Dumbarton Castle, which played important roles in the history of medieval Scotland and of Mary, Queen of Scots.

Eamont Bridge

This village close to Penrith is the site of a Neolithic henge (that is, circular enclosure) known as King Arthur's Round Table. The henge consists of banks and ditches in a circular form, hence its name. It dates from between 2000 and 1000 BC and according to local tradition was King Arthur's jousting arena.

Loch Arthur

This small loch, close to the A711 as it runs southwest from Dumfries, is the most northern of the putative Excalibur lakes. The lake is surrounded by hills and woods and although locals claim that King Arthur's sword rests on the bottom of the loch, only the name makes any connection with King Arthur.

Loch Lomond

One of the great scenic lochs of the Highlands – and the most accessible from Glasgow – Loch Lomond appears in the narrative of Geoffrey of Monmouth, who tells of an offensive by Arthur against the Picts and Scots here. He tells of how Arthur and his army,

> reached Loch Lomond [and] took possession of the islands in the lake, hoping to find a safe refuge on them … Arthur collected together a fleet of boats and sailed round the rivers. By besieging his enemies for fifteen days, he reduced them to such as state of famine that they died in their thousands.

Geoffrey describes the loch as being fed by sixty rivers and having sixty islands, each with sixty eagle's nests – a description that was taken from the earlier *Mirabilia*.

Longtown

Longtown is a village 6 miles from Carlisle on the English-Scottish border. The Church of St Michael and All Angels, on the outskirts of the village, is built on the site of a sixth-century church and is known as the 'Arthuret Church'. The derivation of this name is obscure but might arise from the fact that the site of the church overlooks a suggested site for the Battle of Arfderydd, fought in 573, mention of which appears in Geoffrey of Monmouth's *Vita Merlini* and in the *Annales Cambriae*. The battle was fought between the warlord Gwenddoleu ap Ceidio and his cousins Peredur and Gwrgi, who seem to be princes either from York or Gwynedd. In the battle Myrddin (Merlin) kills his nephew, who is fighting on the opposing side; this act drives Myrddin mad and he spends the rest of his life roaming the forests of Celyddon. Local tradition claims Arthur was buried in the church after the battle of Camlann, which was fought at Birdoswald (see above). The Arthurian connections are celebrated in a caravan park named Camelot about a quarter of a mile from Arthuret.

Meigle

Situated just north of Perth, the churchyard in this village features a plaque identifying a mound as 'Vanora's Mound' – the grave of Guinevere. Local legend maintains that Guinevere made her way to Scotland after the death of King Arthur and changed her name to Vanora or Ganore (meaning 'wanderer'). But the townsfolk of Meigle disliked her lustful ways and killed her.

Mote of Mark

This hill on the coastline of Dumfries and Galloway rises above the village of Rockcliffe and looks out over an inlet known as Rough Firth. The fort at its summit was occupied from the fifth to the seventh centuries, and it is this that gives it the possible connection with King Arthur. Excavations in 1913 and 1973 unearthed a large, circular timber hut, evidence of metalworking, and items of ceramics and glassware from Europe, indicating extensive trading links.

Pendragon Castle

This castle at Mallerstang, situated 4 miles south of Kirkby Stephen in Cumbria, was founded by William the Conqueror's son and successor, William Rufus. The castle is built on an artificial mound close to the River Eden and the present structure on the site, which is ruined, was built by Hugh de Morville, one of the assassins who murdered Thomas a Becket in Canterbury Cathedral. Legend tells that William Rufus's castle was built over the ruins of a previous castle that belonged to Uther Pendragon, the father of King Arthur, who diverted the River Eden to make a moat around the castle. Abandoned earthworks and entrenchments around the castle mound have probably given rise to this story.

Richmond Castle

The ruins of Richmond Castle overlook the River Swale in the North Yorkshire town of Richmond. Legend tells that the castle was built over the entrance to a hidden chamber in which Arthur and his knights lay sleeping. A local potter, named Thompson, is said to have discovered

Pendragon Castle near Kirkby Stephen is the legendary seat of Arthur's father, Uther Pendragon. (*Source, Wikimedia Commons*)

the entrance to the cavern and, on entering, found King Arthur and his knights sleeping around a Round Table. On the table lay a mighty sword and an ancient horn, and when the potter reached out and picked up the ancient horn, the sleepers began to awake. He fled in terror, and heard a voice behind him decrying his actions. 'Potter Thompson, Potter Thompson!' the voice admonished him. 'If thou hadst drawn the sword or blown the horn / Thou hadst been the luckiest man e'er was born!' But Thompson had done neither; he had just picked up the horn, rather than blowing it or drawing the sword – and so remained unlucky.

Sewingshields

The castle located on the site of this fort on Hadrian's Wall was levelled during the nineteenth century and no trace of it remains. Legend tells that a local farmer found the entrance to a cave here, hidden among the castle ruins, and inside he found Arthur and his court asleep. The rest of the legend follows a similar line to the story associated with Richmond Castle. On a table the farmer sees a garter, a sword and a bugle. Arthur and his knights will arise if the garter is cut and the bugle is blown. The farmer cuts the garter with the sword but does not blow the bugle, and Arthur wakes, berating him with the words, 'O woe betide that evil day / On which this witless wight was born! / Who drew the sword, the garter cut / But never blew the bugle-horn.'

Slack

This former Roman fort near Huddersfield is believed by some to be the site of Camelot (discussed on p.126).

Stirling

It is said that King Arthur and his knights used to meet at a huge stone slab in Stirling, which has since disappeared. The source of this legend might be the chronicler William Worcester, who wrote in 1478 that 'King Arthur kept the Round Table at Stirling Castle' – though where he got this association from is unclear. The King's Knot is a series of octagonal-shaped earthworks close to the southwest walls of Stirling Castle and is known locally as King Arthur's Round Table; however the formations are not very old, being the last vestige of a formal garden dating from 1627. At their centre is a flat-topped central mound, 45 ft in diameter and around 6 ft high, which might be older than the other formations.

Arthurian Sites in Southeast England

Colchester

Largely because of its Roman connections, Colchester has been claimed by some to be the original Camelot (see p.125-126).

The London Stone

This ancient, mystical stone can be viewed outside a building across the road from Cannon Street station in the City of London. Legends identify it as the stone from which the boy Arthur pulled the sword, thus anointing him as king (discussed on p.40-41).

Arthurian Sites in Continental Europe

Mont St Michel, Brittany

This famous island, which is attached to the mainland by a short causeway, is situated on the coast of north-west France exactly where Normandy and Brittany meet, and is home to an abbey that was founded in the eighth century. The buildings are an eclectic mix of Romanesque and Gothic styles and form the most familiar profile in France besides the Eifel Tower; they are swarmed over by hundreds of thousands of tourists every year, whose presence in such large numbers somewhat diminishes the atmosphere of this otherwise serene place, particularly at busy times.

According to Geoffrey of Monmouth's *Historia*, after his coronation Arthur began a campaign against the Romans that saw him cross the Channel to Brittany, where he received some startling news.

> A giant of monstrous size was come from the shores of Spain, and had forcibly taken away Hélène, the niece of Duke Hoel [Arthur's nephew, who was King of Brittany] from her guard, and fled with her to the top of that which is now called Michael's Mount ... the soldiers of the country who pursued him were able to do nothing against him. For whether they

Mont St Michel in Brittany, where - as at St Michael's Mount in Cornwall - Arthur is reputed to have slain a giant. (*Source, Antoine Lamielle, Wikimedia Commons*)

attacked him by sea or land, he either overturned their ships with vast rocks, or killed them with several sorts of darts, besides many of them that he took and devoured half alive.

One of Arthur's kinsmen, Bedver, then encounters a woman wailing with grief at the summit of a nearby mountain. She is discovered to be the nurse of Hélène, who is lamenting at Hélène's grave – for she has been killed by the giant. The nurse issues a warning to Bedver:

> O, unhappy man, what misfortune brings you to this place? O the inexpressible tortures of death that you must suffer! I pity you, I pity you, because the detestable monster will this night destroy the flower of your youth. For that most wicked and odious giant, who brought the duke's niece, whom I have just now buried here, and me, her nurse, along with her into this mountain, will come and immediately murder you in a most cruel manner. O deplorable fate! This most illustrious princess, sinking under the fear her tender heart conceived, while the foul monster would have embraced her, fainted away and expired. And when he could not satiate his brutish lust upon her, who was the very soul, joy, and happiness of my life, being enraged at the disappointment of his bestial desire, he forcibly committed a rape upon me, who (let God and my old age witness) abhorred his embraces. Fly, dear sir, fly, for fear he may come, as he usually does, to lie with me, and finding you here most barbarously butcher you!

Bedver says he will get help, and returns to Arthur, who fights and kills the giant. 'He gave the giant no respite till he had struck it up to the very back through his skull,' Geoffrey's narrative relates. 'At this the hideous monster raised a dreadful roar, and like an oak torn up from the roots by the winds, so did he make the ground resound with his fall. Arthur, bursting out into a fit of laughter at the sight, commanded Bedver to cut off his head, and give it to one of the armour-bearers, who was to carry it to the camp, and there expose it to public view.' Hélène was buried on the island of Tombelaine, which is now a bird reserve and at low tide can be reached on foot (with a guide) from Mont Saint-Michel. The name of the island might derive from 'the tomb of Hélène', though other derivations include the Celtic for 'a little mountain' or a reference to a Celtic god.

Mount Etna

Southern Italy might seem a strange place to have a strong connection with Arthurian legend. But in the eleventh century it was ruled by the Normans, who brought tales of King Arthur to this part of the Mediterranean from their newly conquered territory of England. The legends revolve around the breathtaking mirages that appear over the narrow Strait of Messina, which divides Sicily from the mainland of Italy. Known as Fata Morgana, these mirages are often incredibly detailed and can lead to the reflection of entire cities onto the surface of the water. The phenomenon is named for Morgan le Fay, a supernatural being (or water nymph) who is closely associated with the conjuring of illusions. In the Vulgate *Lancelot* stories she is said to be the Queen of Sicily and is associated with the Pergusa Lake in the centre of the island, which has a number of myths attached to it. According to other legends, Arthur and his knights rest deep within Mount Etna, on the island's east coast, where they guard the Holy Grail under the supernatural protection of Morgan. They are waiting until, once again, their people need them; Arthur sustains himself by taking a single sip from the Grail every year. In the 1220s the Sicily-based legends of Arthur were developed in prose form by the lawyer, stateman and writer Gervase of Tilbury, who had served in the court of the King of Sicily. In his narrative the groom of an Italian bishop follows a stray horse on Mount Etna and comes across Arthur living in a sort of earthly paradise (closely resembling Avalon), entered through a cleft in the rock.

Paimpont Forest

This forest west of Rennes is said to be the Brocéliande Forest of the Arthurian Romances; a lakeside chateau at Concoret is home to the family-oriented Centre de l'Imaginaire Arthurien, featuring pageants, exhibitions and the like (Covered on p.16-17).

Podstrana, Croatia

One theory about the origins of the King Arthur legend is that he is based on a soldier and administrator named L Artorius Castus, who served in Dalmatia (modern-day Croatia) before being transferred to Britain. The theory was championed by the American linguist Kemp Malone who had studied inscriptions found on blocks used in around 1840 to construct parts of St Martin's Church which stands southeast of Podstrana (ancient Pituntini) on the coast of Croatia, some 5 miles from the port town of Split. The inscriptions commemorate the career of Artorius Castus. 'In general,' Kemp wrote in 1925, 'the pseudo-historical Arthur (as distinguished from the Arthur of romance) corresponds with astonishing accuracy to the Artorius of our inscription.' He suggested that the body of Arthurian tales were developed in Sarmatia, an area encompassing parts of modern-day Ukraine, Romania and Hungary, and which stretches east as far as the Caspian Sea, and came to Britain via Sarmatian soldiers who served with Artorius Castus from AD 175 onwards. One of the places in which they served was Ribchester on the River Ribble. Castus himself was serving in York around AD 160 and is the only Roman named Artorius known to have led troops in Britain; he also defended Britain against Barbarian invaders from the North, and led British armies on campaign in Gaul – so did a collective memory of his battles against the Scots become transposed in legend into battles against the Saxons? Whatever the case, Podstrana has developed something of a minor King Arthur souvenir industry, while the hilt of a huge stone sword sticks out of the ground beside the beach, as if waiting to be yanked out by a giant Arthur.

Bibliography and Further Reading

Anon. and Sioned Davies (trans.), *The Mabinogion,* Oxford University Press, 2008; (originally written in the eleventh century).

Anon, *The Awntyrs off Arthure at the Terne Wathelyne: Arthur's adventures at Tarn Wadling: a northern Middle English romance set in Inglewood Forest,* University of Lancaster Department of English, 1988; (originally written around 1400).

Ashe, Geoffrey, *The Discovery of King Arthur,* The History Press, Stroud, 2005; (originally published 1985).

Ashe, Geoffrey, *King Arthur's Avalon: The Story of Glastonbury,* Sutton Publishing, Stroud, 2013; (originally published 1957).

Barber, Richard, *King Arthur: Hero and Legend,* The Boydell Press, Woodbridge, Suffolk, 2004; (originally published as *Arthur of Albion* in 1961).

Batey, Colleen E., *Tintagel Castle,* English Heritage, 2016; (originally published 2010).

Bede, and Judith McClure and Roger Collins (eds) and Bertram Colgrave (trans.), *The Ecclesiastical History of the English People,* Oxford University Press, 2008; (originally written around 730).

Béroul, and Alan S. Fedrick (ed.), *The Romance of Tristan,* Penguin Books, 1978; (originally written in the mid-twelfth century).

Betjeman, John, *Cornwall (Shell Guides),* Faber and Faber, London, 1936 and 1966.

Black, Steve and Scott Lloyd, *The Lost Legend of Arthur: The Untold Story of Britain's Greatest Warrior,* Rider, London, 2002.

Camden, William, *Britannia,* Nabu Press, Charleston, 2014; (originally published 1586).

Carew, Richard, *Survey of Cornwall,* Devon and Cornwall Record Society, 2004; (originally published 1603).

Cowper Powys, John, *Porius,* Duckworth, London, 2007; (originally published 1951).

Cowper Powys, John, *A Glastonbury Romance*, The Powys Society, 2019; (originally published 1932).

Cornwell, Bernard, *The Winter King: A Novel of Arthur,* Michael Joseph, London, 1995.

De Boron, Robert and Nigel Bryant (trans.), *Merlin and the Grail: Joseph of Arimathea, Merlin, Perceval: The Trilogy of Arthurian Prose Romances attributed to Robert de Boron* D.S. Brewer, Cambridge, 2015; (originally written in the twelfth century).

De Troyes, Chrétien and Burton Raffel (trans.), *Lancelot: The Knight of the Cart,* Yale University Press, 1997; (originally written in the twelfth century).

De Troyes, Chrétien and Bryant, Nigel (trans.), *The Complete Story of the Grail* D.S. Brewer, Cambridge, 2015; (originally written around 1190).

Dickinson, L.J., *The Story of King Arthur in Cornwall*, self-published, 1939.

Duncan, Ronald, *Devon and Cornwall,* Batsford, London, 1966.

Dunning, R.W., *Arthur: The King in the West*, Amberley Publishing, Stroud, 2013; (originally published 2009).

Duxbury, Brenda, Michael Williams and Colin Wilson, *King Arthur Country in Cornwall: The Search for the Real Arthur,* Bossiney Books, Bodmin, 1979.

Geoffrey of Monmouth with Michael D. Reeve and Neil Wright, *The History of the Kings of Britain: An Edition and Translation of the De gestis Britonum (Historia Regum Britanniae)*, Boydell Press, Woodbridge, 2007; (originally published around 1136).

Geoffrey of Monmouth *The Life of Merlin, Vita Merlini*, ReadaClassic.com, 2011; (originally written around 1155).

Gerald of Wales and Bartlett, Robert (ed.), *Liber de Principis instructione,* (Oxford University Press, 2018; originally published 1193).

Gildas, and Hugh Alders Williams (trans.), *De Excidio Britanniae; Or, the Ruin of Britain,* Dodo Press, London, 2010; (originally published in the sixth century).

Gossip, James and Ann Preston-Jones, *Worthyvale Inscribed Stone: Archaeological Assessment and Recording*, Cornwall Archaeological Unit, Truro, 2018.

Harper, Charles G., *The Cornish Coast*, Nabu Press, Charleston, 2010; (originally published 1910).

Higham, Nicholas J., *King Arthur: the Making of the Legend*, Yale University Press, 2018.

Howells, Caleb, *King Arthur: The Man Who Conquered Europe*, Amberley Publishing, Stroud, 2019.

James, Edward, *Britain in the First Millennium*, Bloomsbury Academic, London, 2000.

Keegan, Simon *Pennine Dragon: The Real King Arthur of the North*, Newhaven Publishing, Brighton, 2016.

Lacy, Norris J, *The Arthurian Handbook: Second Edition*, Routledge, Abingdon, 2013; (originally published 1997).

Lancelyn Green, Roger, *King Arthur and His Knights of the Round Table* Puffin Classics, London, 2008; (originally published 1953).

Lanier, Sydney, *The Boy's King Arthur*, CreateSpace Independent Publishing 2016; (originally published 1880).

Layamon, *Brut*, CreateSpace Independent Publishing, 2014; (originally written around 1190).

Leland, John, *The Itinerary of John Leland in or About the Years 1535–1543*, Leopold Classic Library, South Yarra, Victoria, 2016; (originally published in the mid sixteenth century).

Lupack, Alan, *The Oxford Guide to Arthurian Literature*, Oxford University Press, 2005.

Malory, Thomas (author) and Helen Cooper (ed.), *Le Morte d'Arthur*, Oxford University Press, 2008; (originally published 1470).

Mason, John *King Arthur's Britain*, MHB Press, 2012.

Matthews, John and Caitlin Matthews, *The Complete King Arthur: Many Faces, One Hero*, Inner Traditions, Rochester, Vermont, 2017.

Mee, Arthur, *The King's England: Cornwall*, Hodder and Stoughton, London, 1967; (originally published 1937).

Morris, John, *The Age of Arthur*, Weidenfeld and Nicholson, London, 2004; (originally published 1973).

Padel, O.J., *Arthur in Medieval Welsh Literature*, University of Wales Press, 2013; (originally published 2000).

Peach, Wystan, *Stonehenge: a New Theory*, self-published, 1961.

Polsue, Joseph, *A Complete Parochial History of the County of Cornwall*, Nabu Press, Charleston, 2013; (originally published 1867).

Steinbeck, John, *The Acts of King Arthur and his Noble Knights*, Penguin Modern Classics, London, 2001; (originally published 1976).

Tennyson, Alfred Lord, *Idylls of the King*, Penguin 1983; (originally published in 1874).

Twain, Mark, *A Connecticut Yankee in King Arthur's Court*, CreateSpace Independent Publishing, 2016; (originally published 1889).

Sullivan, Tony, *King Arthur: Man or Myth*, Pen and Sword Publishing, Barnsley, 2020.

Wace, *Arthurian Chronicles: Roman de Brut*, CreateSpace Independent Publishing, 2015; (originally written around 1155).

White, Paul, *King Arthur's Footsteps*, Bossiney Books, Leeds, 2002.

White, T.H., *The Once and Future King*, (includes *The Sword in the Stone* and following volumes) HarperVoyager, London, 2015; (original volumes published from 1938 onwards).

White, T.H., *The Sword in the Stone,* Harper Collins, London, 2008; (originally published 1938).

William of Malmesbury (author), R.A.B.Mynors, R.M. Thomson and M. Winterbottom (eds), *Gesta Regum Anglorum* (Deeds of the English Kings), Oxford University Press, 1998; (originally written in the twelfth century).

Zimmer Bradley, Marion, *The Mists of Avalon*, Penguin, London, 1993; (originally published 1983).

Index